An Apple A Day

100 Quick Devotionals
When Pressed for Time

Vanessa R. Reynolds M.D.

ISBN: 1501073362
ISBN 13: 9781501073366

To Larry

Thank you for thirty-six years of love and support, even in my most unlovable moments. You are my soul mate, and I can't imagine doing life without you. I don't know which blessings God has in store for us in the years to come, but I look forward to sharing them all with you.

To Jared, Jenna, Justin, Jade, and Jason

I'm proud to be your mother. You all will always be my greatest accomplishments in life. God has placed so much in each of you that I can hardly wait to see the blessings you each will be in the kingdom of God. I'm privileged that I've had the opportunity to watch each of you bloom.
I love you.

To Amanda

My first daughter-in-love, you are a blessing. Thank you for loving my son. God definitely found Jared's one and only helpmate in you. You have encouraged me from the day we met, and as I get to know you more and more, that special gift of God in you is more and more evident.

To Mom and Martin

Thank you for loving me. Thank you for being wonderful parents and grandparents and babysitting so I could write this book! You helped me believe in me and have always supported me in all of my endeavors. I love you both.

Contents

Contents

Contents

Acknowledgments

For seventeen years I've been a member of the Rock Church and World Outreach Center. I couldn't have written this book if I hadn't grown in wisdom from the teachings of this ministry. This book also would not have become a reality without the encouragement my pastors have always given me.

When I first came to "The Rock," I never dreamed I'd be confident enough to speak in front of large audiences. I had three young children and started working in the nursery, rocking babies to sleep. When I met Pastor Deborah Cobrae, she showed me the love of God. She saw in me what I was unable to see. She encouraged me to share my testimony in the women's ministry and took me with her on her travels to teach women all over the world.

Pastor Jim and Pastor Deborah, thank you for always teaching the word, "line upon line, and precept upon precept" as Pastor Jim says every Sunday. Thank you for trusting me to teach the word to the people God has entrusted you with in the women's ministry and at the Rock Bible College. Thank you for ordaining me as a minister of God. I love you both because you taught me how to love God more.

Introduction

Many books use the word of God to inspire and teach people how to live abundant lives. I wrote this book with the same goal in mind but from a different perspective. As a Christian, a black woman, a physician, an ordained minister, a mother, a wife, and a speaker, I feel my life experiences are unique. I believe I can touch a readership that has unknowingly allowed society, prejudices, their families, and ultimately Satan to keep them from truly knowing who they are in Christ. I too was deceived, but I've learned how to live an abundant life, trusting God despite the color of my skin, my sex, or criticism of my faith. I don't have all the answers, but I want to share a few things I've learned in my past fifty-five years of life, thirty years of marriage, 26 years of child rearing, and twenty years of ministry to help others so they don't fall into the same pits I fell into on this road called life.

The mini devotionals in this book—apples, if you will—are ways to keep God in our busy lives. For days when we have a little more time, I've started with what I call "small entrées." Many events and people have shaped who I am. I could talk about the miracle of my admission to medical school, the miracle of my marrying my husband, the miracle of my traveling to Tanzania in East Africa or the Philippines, but in the five short teachings in the first section of this book, I want to share how the births and adoptions of my children shaped my life and ultimately strengthened my faith. Hopefully you can apply the principles God taught me during these years to your own life.

The births and adoptions of my children resulted in far more than additions to our family. They were life lessons God used to place my feet where He would have them go. Jared Michael taught me the importance of praise. Jenna Mishon taught me that God loves me for me and is faithful.

Justin Matthias taught me that God is a jealous God and that I always should put Him first. Jason Marcel taught me how to love others. Jade Michaela taught me self-sacrifice.

I pray that the following five short testimonies, as well as the devotionals in this book, bless your life and help you reflect on the goodness of God as you grow spiritually.

PART ONE

Small Entrées

My Testimonies

The Power of Praise

My oldest son, Jared Michael, taught me a lesson that helped me through many obstacles I faced later in life. Remember, we serve a supernatural God! When everything else is black or white, and one plus one always equals two, with God anything goes.

I was a resident in my last year of emergency medicine and decided (because I have a type A personality and like to plan everything to a tee) that it was time for me to have a baby. This plan was perfect because I would finish my residency and have time to have a child then take a few months off before starting my new job in California.

I was raised in the Baptist church, and when I got my least-desired residency match in emergency medicine in Greenville, North Carolina, my husband Larry and I chose to attend a nondenominational church with a lot of Pentecostal overtones. (For those unfamiliar with the way things work after medical school, there's a process called "Match Day." Medical students interview at different residency programs and rank them in their order of preference; meanwhile the programs also rank the students in their order of preference. At the end of the process, all preferences are placed into a computer program, and the medical students are "matched.") The church we were attending definitely was a teaching ministry, which we loved; therefore we decided we would endure what we considered to be emotionalism during the services. The dancing and singing and the crying out to God, in my mind, were only delaying my learning more about the word of God.

Larry and I became very close with the senior pastor and his wife, sharing Sunday meals with them and learning how God had sustained them through many years of marriage, health concerns, and ministry. They quickly became our spiritual mentors and friends, and we respected their relationships with God as well as their wisdom. When I found out I was pregnant—which came as no surprise because I had planned it, using an ovulation-predictor kit—I was elated that everything was going according to my plan. I thanked God for blessing *my* plan and went on my merry way.

One Sunday evening, as I was enduring an emotional praise-and-worship service, anxious to be taught the word of God, I saw Larry doing a little jig to the song the choir was singing. I thought, *what is he doing?* When the song and music stopped, Larry was still dancing. I was so embarrassed! I was six or seven months pregnant and totally unfamiliar with this kind of emotional display in church. I looked to one of our pastors, and he told the ushers to let Brother Larry continue because he was working something out in the spirit. This was twenty-five years ago, and Larry was wearing a three-piece suit, which was soaked with sweat. His eyes were closed, and he had a very serious look on his face. He continued to dance throughout the sermon, as if he heard music during the entire service, and well after the congregation had left.

I asked my pastors what they felt was going on with him as we sat there in an empty church and watched him dance. They felt he was battling something in the spirit realm, and we should let him work it out. Finally Larry collapsed on the floor and lay there smiling. A few moments later, he opened his eyes, looked up at us, and said, "The baby is going to be OK." I just stared at him in amazement because he had embarrassed himself and me, doing that silly dance in front of everyone during the entire service, and to my knowledge, there was nothing wrong with the baby I was carrying. I thought, *Well, that's good to know. Now let's get home because I have to work in the morning.*

Around one in the morning, I began to have regular contractions—even though I was only twenty-six weeks pregnant—and had to go to the hospital. The doctors told me I was effaced and dilated to two centimeters. They were going to admit me to the hospital to try to stop my contractions long enough so my child could develop further. If I delivered him that night—and if he weighed at least five hundred grams—they were prepared to transport him by helicopter to the nearest neonatal intensive-care unit in the area. When I suddenly remembered Larry's words and how he had humbled himself and danced before the Lord in spiritual warfare, I knew the baby would be OK.

I was in residency at the hospital where I was admitted, so everyone there knew me. They came to visit with solemn faces and told me how sorry they were that I was losing the baby. I reassured them that God had told my husband that our baby was going to be fine. They looked at me sadly, assuming I was in denial of the facts.

The church had someone with me almost constantly, interceding and praying and helping me to stay in faith. An ultrasound was performed on me and showed a large fibroid, which the doctor's thought was causing the premature labor. The neonatal team came in one day to explain what would happen with my preemie as well as the mental abnormalities and bleeding into the baby's brain that I could expect. I told them my baby was going to be OK. When psychiatric workers came to speak to me about "reality" and acceptance of the facts, I told them the same thing.

After a few days of prayer and positive confession, the contractions stopped. Another ultrasound was performed, but now the doctors couldn't find the fibroid. They wanted to send me home with orders for strict bed rest until the expected delivery in June, which would mean I couldn't complete my residency until the fall. However, I'd already accepted a job in California and was due to start in October. I knew then that God had showed my husband and me as Christians His power—and the power of praise—and had prophesized to us that our firstborn child would be all right. I continued with my residency despite the residency director stating that she didn't want to be responsible for the death of my child.

Jared had a due date of June 28, 1988 and weighed eight pounds and fifteen ounces when he was born on June 29, 1988. He was a healthy, beautiful child and has grown up to be an exceptional young man. He was a straight-A student and graduated cum laude with a bachelor's degree in business marketing and administration. He's also a solo concert pianist and a psalmist who's active in our church, and I believe he has a calling to minister Christ to others in his life. Jared recently married the love of his life, and now I have my first daughter-in-love, Amanda.

Was this just a nice story? A coincidence? You can believe what you want to believe, but I know this was the first of many miracles that God would perform in my life to help me become the woman of God he wanted me to be.

I now know that praise works!

> *I will praise thee O Lord with my whole heart! I will be glad and rejoice in thee. I will sing praises to thy name. O thou Most High. (Ps. 9:1–2)*

I often wonder, *if Larry hadn't humbled himself and danced before the Lord, despite what people thought about him, would there ever have been a Jared Michael?*

> *And at midnight Paul and Silas prayed, and sang praises unto God: and the prisoners heard them. And suddenly there was a great earthquake, so that the foundations of the prison were shaken: and immediately all the doors were opened, and everyone's bands were loosed. (Acts 16:25–26)*

Praise is powerful! Paul and Silas were imprisoned, but when they sang praises to God, a great earthquake shook the foundations of the prison, opened the doors to their cell, and released them from their shackles.

> *By him therefore let us offer the sacrifice of praise to God continually, that is, the fruit of our lips giving thanks to his name. (Heb. 13:15)*

> *Let everything that has breath praise the Lord. (Ps. 150:6)*

Praise fights against the Devil, silencing the foe and the avenger. Praise is like a double-edged sword you hold in your hand.

From the lips of children and infants you have ordained praise because of your enemies, to silence the foe and the avenger. (Ps. 8:2 NIV)

Let the saints be joyful in glory; Let them sing aloud on their beds. Let the high praises of God be in their mouth, and a two-edged sword in their hand (Ps. 149:5–6)

Praise the Lord! Praise God in His sanctuary; Praise Him in His mighty firmament! Praise Him for His mighty acts; Praise Him according to His excellent greatness! Praise Him with the sound of the trumpet; Praise Him with the flute and harp! Praise Him with the timbrel and dance; Praise Him with stringed instruments and flutes! Praise Him with loud cymbals; Praise Him with clashing cymbals! Let everything that has breath praise the Lord. Praise the Lord! (Ps. 150:1–6)

. . . .

Life lesson: Take the problem off yourself, your circumstances, and your drama. Stop living in pride. Instead humble yourself enough to realize that all you are and all you have is because of God, and praise Him!

. . . .

Notes:

_____

_____

_____

_____

_____

_____

_____

_____

God Is Faithful

Almost twenty-four years ago, while Jared was growing up, and I was practicing in a busy emergency department, I became pregnant with Jenna Mishon. I named my children before their births and even before they were conceived. I wanted to speak aloud to the individuals whom I believed God wanted them to be, every day of their lives. The name "Jenna" means "heaven," and the Hebrew translation is "Yahweh is gracious and merciful." "Mishon" means "Who is like God?"

I prayed to God for a happy, uneventful pregnancy, and he answered me! Why are we sometimes shocked when our prayers are answered? Maybe we didn't practice as much faith as we'd thought, or perhaps we were praying out of habit, forgetting that we serve a living God who hears and answers us. Unlike my pregnancy with Jared, I carried Jenna to term without complications. I had a wonderful pregnancy as I prepared for my little girl. She was born at 3:23 p.m. on Valentine's Day. Our family's lives and our Valentine's Days have never been the same since 1991.

Jenna's birth was pivotal to the change that God was making in my heart and my self-esteem. My parents were divorced when I was five years old. My father, an alcoholic, determined that marriage wasn't for him. My dysfunctional character trait of approval seeking and my uneasiness around other people were problems I was aware of and unsuccessfully had prayed for deliverance from in the past. (I've since learned these are common traits of children of an alcoholic parent.) I suffered low self-esteem from experiencing racism, not having as much money as my peers had, wearing handmade or thrift-store clothes when I was a child, growing up with an alcoholic father, having a large gap between my front teeth, and perceiving I wasn't attractive, based on the standards of beauty portrayed on television and in magazines.

Jenna was born at a time when I needed reassurance that God loved me for me and that His faithfulness was assured forever. My mother had worked relentlessly to provide for me, her only child. Her studies were disrupted when she was married at age fifteen, and when she was seventeen, she gave birth to me. When I was in elementary school, she obtained her GED and then her bachelor's degree.

For my entire life, I had carried the past like a weight on my shoulders. In high school I was rude and unfriendly to strangers as a defense mechanism to prevent myself from being bullied or hurt. I had accepted Jesus as Lord in middle school, but I had failed to allow the changes that rightfully should occur when a daughter of the King of Kings and Lord of Lords is adopted into His family. Even as an adult, I didn't realize who I was in Christ and still believed what I'd been told—what society characterized me as being. In my eyes I was inadequate.

The fact that Jenna's birth and pregnancy were uneventful was the miracle I needed. I'd been seeking God to discover His plan for my life. I was slowly growing spiritually, but because of my past, I couldn't understand the love of God. Psalm 37:4 states, "Delight yourself also in the Lord, and He shall give you the desires of your heart." I knew the verse in my head, but it didn't move from my head to my heart until Jenna was born. It finally clicked that God really loved *me* so much that He had died for me, and He wanted to give me the desires of my heart. My desire was a beautiful daughter, and as I grew in the Lord, he took away the pain of the past, and I began to truly be a new creature in Christ. I realized God trusted me with this little girl because I was valuable in His eyes. Jenna was such a wonderful, happy baby and a joy to be around that she helped me finally know the love of God. The fact that God loved me more than I loved this beautiful baby girl—whom I loved with all my heart—made me stop hating myself so I could fully love her.

Raising Jenna every day reminded me that I was what the word of God said I was: wonderfully and beautifully made, regardless of society's standards. As she grew, her personality and sense of humor kept everyone laughing and happy despite any problems we faced. Today Jenna is a concert pianist who graduated from Texas Christian University with a bachelor's degree in communications and a minor in music. She delights our family with her humor and wit, and I can't imagine life without her. She's heaven for Larry and me and follows after God, as her name suggests. We thank Him for His mercy and grace for allowing us to raise her to be the lovely young woman she has become. After Jenna was born, I had a new purpose in life because God miraculously, in a moment, took away my low self-esteem and placed me on the path to learn to love.

Many people have endured less-than-happy experiences in the past, and they lug them around for the rest of their lives. Jesus wants us to realize that He's here to carry the load. He asks us to cast our cares on Him, whatever they are. Whether you were born as a result of an encounter between two drunken parents who didn't know each other, were dumped into a trashcan after your first breath of life, or had alcoholic or abusive parents, God loves you!

God is not a man, that He should lie, nor a son of man, that He should repent; Has He said, and will He not do it? Or has He spoken, and will He not make it good? (Num. 23:19 ESV)

I wonder how many people never achieve all that God has planned for them because their low self-esteem or past hurts hold them back. God has proved his faithfulness time and time again in his word. Hebrews 11 speaks about God's faithfulness to Noah, Abraham, Sarah, Moses, and Rahab, just to name a few. He is not a respecter of persons, and He does not lie. If God came through for them, He will come through for you.

The Lord's loving kindnesses indeed never cease, For His compassions never fail. They are new every morning; Great is Your faithfulness. (Lam. 3:22–23 NAS)

And being fully assured that what God had promised, He was able also to perform. (Rom. 4:21 NAS)

Life lesson: You are wonderfully and beautifully made, and God has a specific plan and purpose for your life. You have a new Father in heaven regardless of the one you were given on earth. Don't allow the enemy to steal one more moment of your happiness. Give God the cares of this world, and begin life afresh, walking in His plan for you.

Notes:

God Is Jealous

I'd always wanted three children; I was thirty-five and ready to have my third. I felt I had the formula down by now—I'd use an ovulation-predictor kit and pray that God would bless my plans so I could stay on track with *my* life desires.

I wasn't at all shocked when I found out I was pregnant with our third child. I was very shocked—and quite devastated—however, when I found out at twelve weeks, during the ultrasound, that the baby had no heartbeat. After mourning I found out Larry and I could try again in six months, so I just determined that this snafu was one of life's surprises, and I wouldn't dwell on it but move on.

My logic began to fail when this scenario repeated itself with another pregnancy and yet another. I couldn't go anywhere without seeing children and pregnant women; my pregnancy schedule was entirely messed up; and I couldn't figure out why this kept happening. I kept wondering whether God was angry with me or whether I was doing something wrong. Well, the doctors at that time felt I probably had a secondary form of infertility because of all the miscarriages, followed by dilations and curettages (also known as "D&Cs"). My doctors thought my D&Cs from multiple miscarriages had scarred my uterine lining and were interfering with pregnancy implantation. They told me I could have no more children.

The Bible asks, "Whose report will you believe?" in Isaiah 53:1 Often we're given a choice of believing what scientists or people we respect in our family put before us or believing the word of God. In our finite minds, however, the word of God doesn't always make sense. Who can wrap his or her mind around a God who is the Father, Son, and Holy Spirit? Who can fully understand how God can be in multiple places at once, bringing all our prayers to fruition? We understand that all things work together for good for those who love God according to Romans 8:28. Therefore, we pray according to the word, in faith whether we understand God's answer or not.

In their efforts to console me, family and friends pointed out how blessed I was with a beautiful boy and girl and said I should stop putting myself through this time and time again. I sought the Lord in prayer, however, and I believed there would be a Justin Matthias from my womb. "Justin" means "one who is just, upright, and righteous." Matthias was the disciple who was favored to replace Judas; the name means "gift of God." I was obsessed with having a third child. After all, I was a child of God, and this was a desire of my heart, so what could possibly be the problem? I spoke God's word regarding my situation; I had found the specific Bible verses that pertained to what I was going through and confessed them multiple times daily. I prayed and fasted. I asked others to pray with me, because if one person puts a thousand to flight, two will put ten thousand to flight, and I needed an exponential number of prayers to bombard heaven. What was the issue? Why couldn't I carry a child to term?

I didn't understand until later that I was treating God as if He were a genie in a bottle, thinking He would do what I desired if I used the right formula. God, however, is omniscient, omnipresent, omnipotent, and sovereign. You can't serve God and mammon. You can't make your having a child— or anything else in life for that matter—more important than Him. After mourning and weeping and suffering miscarriage after miscarriage, I finally began to pray. For once I stopped praying for this baby, rebuking the Devil, and reminding God of his word. Instead I prayed to be closer to God. I prayed that I would develop a relationship with Him in which I would know His will and hear His voice all the days of my life. I determined in my heart that I would thank Him for the children He had blessed me with, and if I never had another child, I would serve God and love Him just the same. I stopped trying to get pregnant, stopped buying ovulation-predictor kits, and stopped stressing over the entire issue. My peace returned; my joy returned; and lo and behold, I got pregnant with Justin and carried him to term.

Justin Matthias is now a sophomore in college, pursuing a degree in sociology. He's a blessing and a reminder that God is faithful. He plays piano and baseball, is humorous and able to think outside the box, and is truly a gift from God. As a child Justin loved money and called dollar bills "money tickets." He always has been entrepreneurial minded, and as he draws closer to God and matures, I have no doubt that God will use him in ways that provide financial blessings to the kingdom of God.

What have you elevated in your life above God? Children, spouses, jobs, weight loss, exercise, money, friends, electronics, sports, television, and hobbies are just a few things that sometimes compete with God. We must love the Lord our God with all our hearts and souls and with all our strength and have no other gods before Him. If we learn to cast aside our cares, as the Bible teaches, we will worry less and spend more time with God. Matthew 6:33 says, "But seek ye first the kingdom of God and his righteousness, and all these things shall be added unto you." Justin taught me that God is a jealous God and desires to be first in all that we do.

No one can serve two masters, for either he will hate the one and love the other, or he will be devoted to the one and despise the other. You cannot serve God and money. (Matt. 6:24 ESV)

I am the vine; you are the branches. Whoever abides in me and I in him, he it is that bears much fruit, for apart from me you can do nothing. (John 15:5 ESV)

And he said to him, "You shall love the Lord your God with all your heart and with all your soul and with all your mind. (Matt. 22:37 ESV)

And God spoke all these words, saying, "I am the Lord your God, who brought you out of the land of Egypt, out of the house of slavery. You shall have no other gods before me." (Exod. 20:1–3 ESV)

. . . .

Life lesson: Put God first in everything. Nothing on earth is more important than your eternal salvation and the God who provided it for you. Make sure that the cares of this world don't creep in and dominate your thoughts and life. It's so easy to make little gods in your life without even realizing it. We serve a jealous God.

. . . .

Notes:

The Power of Love

Approximately ten years ago, God put in my heart the desire to adopt a child. Our biological children were blessings, and God had blessed our lives so much that I wanted to share our blessings by helping a child who was less fortunate than my own. At that time Larry wasn't in agreement and felt we had enough going on with our own children and couldn't take on more responsibility. Every couple of years, however, I brought up the subject with him because my desire to adopt a child wouldn't go away.

More than 350,000 children in the United States are in the foster-care system. I knew Larry and I couldn't make a dent in that number, but the urge to do something weighed heavily on my heart. How could we—to whom God had given so much—not give back? Finally, after several years, in 2008 Larry said we could look into it. I discussed the possibilities with Jared, Jenna, and Justin, and they all were excited. We knew adopting a child would change our lives forever, but we were all on board. I sought out a Christian adoption agency in our area, and Larry and I began to attend classes. The adoption process can be time-consuming and difficult, but because there's such a need for adoptive families, the agency helped expedite the process. After evening and weekend classes, CPR and basic life-support (BLS) training, and home visits, we were official. All adoptive parents in California must start as foster parents. Larry and I received short bios and photographs of the children we could meet. We were to choose a child then go to the social-services office to meet him or her and determine whether we wanted a weekend visit with the child in our home.

Jason was one of the first five children whose information and photograph we received, and Larry and I immediately knew from his picture that he was to be a part of our family. Because all our children had the same initials ("J.M."), we wanted to change his name entirely to match our biological children's initials. His new name became Jason Marcel (Jason means "the healer," and "Marcel" means "little warrior"). I wanted this child to be healed from all the pain of his past, and I knew he needed to fight to do it. Larry and I named him before we met him.

Prior to our first visit with Jason, social services told us he didn't speak much, and his current foster mom thought he might have learning problems. Our entire family prayed about whether we should pursue adopting Jason, and this information didn't deter us. Jason Marcel was officially to be a Reynolds. When Larry and I met him, we realized that everything we had heard about him was untrue. He was a bright, happy two-year-old boy. We played with blocks with him and read him stories. He obviously was following the pictures and was engaged with us. It was truly love at first sight. I felt my heart grow at that moment; I felt the love of Christ and a peace in my spirit that this was my son.

Unfortunately the courts didn't care what my heart was saying. I was just a foster mother. Biweekly parental visits were scheduled, and each time I would pack Jason a lunch and give him to the social worker, who would then drive him one to two hours to see his biological parents. No matter the victories we'd previously overcome, each parental visit caused a major setback. Jason would resume wetting himself and throw tamper tantrums after these visits. The social worker would have to pry each finger from around my neck when he came to take Jason to see his biological parents. Jason would cry and scream, and I cried too. It was so emotionally draining that I sometimes prayed the entire day until the social worker brought him back home.

My command is this: Love each other as I have loved you. (John 15:12)

Praise be to God that at our lowest moments, when we feel we can't handle one more thing, God steps in. He never will give us more than we can handle. He cares about what we care about. It took two years for Larry and me to make it through the entire court process and legally adopt

Jason. We celebrated his adoption day with all our family and friends, but he was a part of our family from the first day we saw him.

When we allow the same love that God showed us by sending His only son to die on the cross for our sins to fill our hearts, we too will be able to love as Christ loved. We must open our hearts to the less fortunate, those in need, and those who are hurting. Remember, there's always someone in a situation that's worse than yours. Let the fruit of the Spirit that God has placed in your heart grow. Above all, love.

A new commandment I give to you, that you love one another, even as I have loved you, that you also love one another. By this all men will know that you are My disciples, if you have love for one another. (John 13:34–35)

Beloved, let us love one another, for love is from God, and whoever loves has been born of God and knows God. Anyone who does not love does not know God, because God is love. (1 John 4:7–8)

. . . .

Life lesson: The love of God will motivate you to do things that may not seem possible. Remembering how much Christ loves us enables us to enlarge our hearts more than we ever might think possible. God is love, and we are His children. This love is in all of us, and we only need that fruit to grow. Water it every day by doing something for someone other than yourself. Let the fruit of the Spirit be large in your life.

. . . .

Notes:

The Power of Obedience

J ason had been with us for about a year when I received a call from social services informing me that he had a full biological sister who was
having problems in her foster home. This child was five years old and had
been with the same foster mom since birth. The social worker asked me
whether we would consider taking her into our home if they had to remove
her from her foster home. I replied that we would pray for God to confirm
in our spirits whether to bring this child into our home.

The family was adjusting, and Jason was adapting nicely, and this new
situation was totally unplanned. I felt like a mom who had just found out
she was pregnant when she and her husband had been using contracep-
tives. I called Larry, who said, "Let's pray about it," but shortly after I got
off the phone with him, social services called and said the police were
going to remove Jason's sister from her preschool at that moment. They
wanted our answer in an hour.

This child had been traumatized and frightened when she had been
taken from the only environment she'd ever known and was placed in social services. If Larry and I agreed, she wouldn't have to go to multiple
foster homes. If we agreed, the biological brother she didn't know existed
and otherwise never would meet would be raised with his sister.

The moment I was asked, I knew the answer before praying. I couldn't
let this little girl go into the system. She deserved to be raised with her
brother. God had a plan and a purpose for her, and He was asking Larry
and I to be obedient and give her a home. We didn't ask for two more children, but God often takes you out of your area of comfort and stretches
you for his kingdom. I prayed with my husband, but all the while, I felt in

my heart, *Not my will, Lord, but your will be done in my life.* There was very little time, and I didn't know how everything would work out. I didn't have a bed, clothes, or toys for the girl. Jason was adjusting well, and I didn't want the introduction of a new child into the home to hinder his progress. Even so, I knew this would become a reality. Larry and I were being given the opportunity to be blessings to one of God's precious gems. When talking to my husband, I didn't realize I already had named her until he pointed it out. Larry and I walked by faith, not knowing any answers, and Jade Michaela became a part of our family. The name "Jade" means "precious gem," and "Michaela" means "gift of God."

The social worker told me Jade would be at our house in two hours, with only the clothes on her back. I ran to the store and bought some essentials I thought would fit her. Besides Jason, my youngest child was fifteen years old, so it had been a while since I'd had a five-year-old at home. I grabbed underwear, pajamas, pants, shirts, socks, and anything else I could find quickly. When Jade arrived that night, it was around nine, and she was asleep. She had cried during the entire drive to our home. Jared carried her to the sofa in our bedroom so that when she woke up, she wouldn't be afraid, and Larry and I would be right there. Around 3:00 a.m. Larry nudged me, and there was Jade standing next to his side of the bed, just looking at us. I said, "Hi, Jade. I'm going to be your new mommy. Do you want to get into the bed with us?" She nodded and jumped into the bed between Larry and me then went back to sleep.

From the first day through the present, Jade has blessed us. Although there have been trials because of her background, she's overcoming them daily and growing into a beautiful, godly young lady. She loves to sing and is taking voice and piano lessons. She accepted Jesus as her personal Lord and Savior last year and loves him with all her heart. She's a born athlete who currently plays soccer. Jade is an outspoken leader, an organizer, and a gifted little girl. I have no doubt she could be president of the United States some day if that is her desire.

Larry and I didn't believe we could open our hearts and home to additional two children and start the child-rearing process all over again, but God touched our hearts, and we were obedient. God honors our obedience. Even when it's difficult, we sometimes must stretch ourselves in order to be obedient to God. He will strengthen you, equip you, and bless you to do the task at hand. Trust him, and don't grow weary in doing good things, because in due time you will reap your harvest.

You are my friends if you do what I command. (John 15:14)

If you love me, you will obey what I command. (John 14:15)

And this is love: that we walk in obedience to his commands. As you have heard from the beginning, his command is that you walk in love. (2 John 1:6)

. . . .

Life lesson: No matter how difficult it may be, obeying God is always the right choice. Trust your heart; obey God's word; and take action. These are steps proven again and again in the Bible that cause blessings to flow. God may be asking you to stretch yourself today. What He's asking may seem an impossibility for you at the time, but He will enable you to be victorious.

. . . .

Notes:

PART TWO

Daily Apples

100 Devotionals

Obeying God at all Cost

For am I now seeking the approval of man or of God? Or am I trying to please man? If I were still trying to please man, I would not be a servant of Christ. (Gal. 1:10 ESV)

We must choose God at all costs. Doing so may cost you some "friends," some family relationships, or your job, but God will bless you when you choose Him. Job was a rich man, and everything was taken from him. Job's wife told him to curse God, but he chose to please God. He lost riches, possessions, and family members, but in the end, God restored twice what he had lost. God will do the same for us when we seek to please Him. So how do you please God? By your faith and obedience. How do you get faith? Hear God's word over and over. How do you obey God's word? It starts one step at a time but requires action on your part. Hear the word, increase your faith, and take action to obey, and you will please God.

Are you more concerned with people's opinion of you, or God's opinion?

What will you change today to be a better witness for Christ?

Milk or Meat?

For though by this time you ought to be teachers, you need someone to teach you again the first principles of the oracles of God; and you have come to need milk and not solid food. (Heb. 5:12 NKJV)

Although milk drinkers hear the word of God, nothing changes in their lives. They keep going to church but don't know how to trust God, or how to use God's word to face everyday trials. They're crying for a bottle and getting fed milk, but they can't be blessings because of their spiritual immaturity. They are taught the same things over and over but never grow. Meat eaters, however, hear God's word and apply it. They face trials but find Scripture, believe God's word, and wait for God to come through with joy. They know God never will give them more than they can bear because God says this is so. Let's make sure we are growing spiritually—eating meat—so God can use us and bless us.

Are you battling the same issues as you were last year this time or have you grown?

Controlling Emotions

A gentle answer deflects anger, but harsh words make tempers flare. (Prov. 15:1 NLT)

Choose your battles in relationships. Ask yourself, *Is this issue worth it, or am I acting out of pride? Are my feelings hurt? Am I offended? Is this why I can't let go of this issue?* When you set pride aside, most conflicts easily can be resolved. If you use your words to hurt someone, and he or she fires back at you, what kind of victory have you won? Having the last word is more of an indication of our own spiritual immaturity. You can say you're sorry with God's help, even if you aren't at fault. If your thoughts are on pleasing and being obedient to God, you can give a gentle answer, even when someone's words are meant to hurt you. Everything we do should be done as if we are doing it unto God. Control the tongue, overcome outbursts of anger, and please God. Blessed are the meek in spirit. This doesn't mean you should be a doormat, but you should be strong enough to control your emotions and fear God.

The next time you begin to feel angry, what are some things you can do before lashing out?

Childlike Faith

The Lord protects those of childlike faith; I was facing death, and he saved me. (Ps. 116:6 NLT)

When children trust you, they believe everything you say. If you tell a child Santa Claus or the tooth fairy exists, he or she will believe you. As we mature we see others' faults and imperfections and question the inconsistencies. Childlike faith requires taking God at His word. If He says He will do it, He will. If He says you can do it, you can. The truth for us as Christians is not what we're told, not what we see, not how we feel but whatever God's word says. Childlike faith brings God's protection just when you need it. Trust God and His word—in the beginning was the word, and the word was God.

List all the times when God has shown his faithfulness to you.

_____

_____

_____

_____

_____

_____

_____

_____

_____

_____

_____

Watch Your Mouth

Today the Lord will conquer you, and I will kill you and cut off your head. And then I will give the dead bodies of your men to the birds and wild animals, and the whole world will know that there is a God in Israel! (1 Sam. 17:46 NLT)

David told the giant what he would do before he did it. This is an example of walking by faith instead of sight. He didn't compare his size with the giant's size or worry that God might not show up. David was confident and spoke what hadn't yet happened as though it were a thing of the past. We must watch our mouths. Regardless of what we see, we must speak the word. The word says we were healed by Jesus's stripes two thousand years ago, even when our bodies feel sick. The word says we can do all things through Christ even when we feel overwhelmed. The word says all our needs are met according to God's riches in glory, even when the bills have piled up. Don't look at the natural circumstances. Trust God's word, which never returns void. Tell your body, tell your doubts, and tell your finances to line up with the word! Speak the word, the truth. God is not man and cannot lie.

What are you believing God for today? Find a scripture to stand on while you wait to see your prayers come to pass. Start speaking the word!

God Given Talents

We must quickly carry out the tasks assigned us by the one who sent us. The night is coming, and then no one can work. (John 9:4 NLT)

Procrastinating often is easier than completing the task at hand. God has placed gifts and passions in us. In addition there's a lost and dying world that does not know Jesus. God has equipped you to use your gifts and passions to love people into the kingdom. Is there something you've thought about doing time after time but talked yourself out of because you felt it would never happen? Start today! Ask God to show you what to do and to open doors that only He can in order to make your dreams a reality. You have been wonderfully and beautifully made, not to just live and die but to make a difference. Can you smile, encourage, teach, cook, sing, work with children, play an instrument, write, tutor, or teach sports? Start using whatever God has given you to be a blessing today.

What are your talents and how can you use them to be a blessing?

Choose Friends Wisely

Proverbs 15:1 NLT
I meant that you are not to associate with anyone who claims to be a believer yet indulges in sexual sin, or is greedy, or worships idols, or is abusive, or is a drunkard, or cheats people. Don't even eat with such people.(1 Corinthians 5:11)

The Apostle Paul inspired by the Holy Spirit wrote this book to the Corinthian church. He was serious about Christians who associated with sinners. He wanted the Christians who lived a lifestyle of sin removed from the fellowship completely. He taught the people that allowing this fellowship to continue would eventually destroy them all. 1 Corinthians 5:6 states "Don't you realize that this sin is like a little yeast that spreads through the whole batch of dough?" The same statement rings true today. We must be very careful in choosing our friends. We must determine whom we choose to hang out with based on the word of God. He isn't talking about judging unbelievers, but believers. Christians, claiming to know Jesus yet obviously not following him by the lifestyle they lead. (Matthew 7:20) Yes, just as you can identify a tree by its fruit, so you can identify people by their actions. Look at their fruit and choose your friends wisely. Make sure you too are producing good fruit that others can see.

Do your friends encourage you to do things that you no longer feel comfortable doing? Do your friends push you more toward the things of God or away from them?

Motives Count

But Samuel replied, "What is more pleasing to the Lord: your burnt offerings and sacrifices or your obedience to his voice? Listen! Obedience is better than sacrifice, and submission is better than offering the fat of rams. (1 Sam. 15:22 NLT)

God told Saul to entirely destroy the Amalekites. Saul chose to destroy them in obedience but kept the best of the sheep and oxen for a sacrifice to God. Saul partially obeyed God, keeping the things he felt were worth keeping instead of destroying everything, as commanded by God. Do you ever partially obey God? Coming to church out of habit or for any reason other than to hear from and worship God—that's partially obeying. Tithing because it's the right thing to do when you're angry that you have to give—that's partially obeying God. Praying a memorized prayer out of habit instead of praying it from your heart—that's partially obeying God. He wants you to do these things because you want to do them, not because it's a habit or ritual. Do the right thing from your heart, or your sacrifices will mean nothing. Check your motives in regard to whatever you do for Jesus. Our obedience is better than our sacrifices to God.

Are there areas of your life where you have partially obeyed God? Have you justified the decisions that you've made, trying to convince yourself of your obedience?

Giants

The Lord who rescued me from the claws of the lion and the bear will rescue me from this Philistine!" Saul finally consented. "All right, go ahead," he said. "And may the Lord be with you!" (1 Sam, 17:37 NLT)

David wasn't afraid of the giant Goliath. With God's help he had defeated a lion and a bear, so he trusted God with this enemy as well. We too have Goliaths in our lives. Illness, depression, debt, pride, anxiety, low self-esteem, addictions, and unforgiveness are just a few. God also has helped you fight some lions and some bears in the past. Take a moment to think of some situations when God showed up on your behalf. Use these memories to increase your faith for the current giants in your life. Remember that God is the same yesterday, today, and forever. He'll do it again! He's faithful! He cares! He loves you so much that He died for you. Take your single stone of faith and your slingshot, and defeat your giants just like David did.

What giants has Jesus helped you slay? What giants are you still believing God to conquer?

Live by the Power of God

For the Kingdom of God is not just a lot of talk; it is living by God's power. (1 Corinthians 4:20)

Living by God's power is about realizing you are in this world but not of this world. Your heavenly father has paved a path for you as a believer in Him that is different than that of the world. He gave his life so that we could be free from sin. He took stripes on his back so we could be healed. He rose again so that we could have our relationship with the father restored. The power we live in is the same power that raised Christ from the grave. The power we live in enables us to believe in the impossible just because God said it. The power we live in allows us to have more than we can dream about or even imagine in this life. This same power gives us hope and the peace that surpasses all understanding for whatever storms in life come our way. This resurrection power is inside of us and because of it we come out of trials victoriously. Don't just say you are a Christian. Instead live this life in the resurrection power of Jesus Christ. Matthew 5:16 In the same way, let your good deeds shine for all to see, so that everyone will praise your heavenly Father.

What have you done in public to honor your heavenly father?

God Will Show Up

"Let's go across to the outpost of those pagans," Jonathan said to his armor bearer. "Perhaps the Lord will help us, for nothing can hinder the Lord. He can win a battle whether he has many warriors or only a few!" (1 Sam. 14:6 NLT)

I love this story because Jonathan had no fear and wholeheartedly trusted God. Who would dare face an entire Philistine army with just one other person? Jonathan risked his life, believing that God would show up. Jonathan and his armor bearer killed about twenty men before confusion broke out in the Philistine camp and their men began to fight and kill one another. God showed up...and with His help, two men defeated an army. Are there battles in your life that seem impossible? The battle is not yours; it's the Lord's. Just as He showed up for Jonathan, He will show up for you. You can't be in fear and faith simultaneously. Trust God!

Do you truly believe that God will show up for the battle that you are facing right now? What verses are you standing on?

Words Give Life

Gentle words are a tree of life; a deceitful tongue crushes the spirit. (Prov. 15:4 NLT)

Be an exhorter! Sticks and stones hurt your bones, but words hurt too. You must watch your tongue. Your tongue is small but powerful. You don't know what others are facing in life. When someone is rude, short-tempered, or unfriendly toward you, there's usually a reason behind it. Words can change someone's entire day, perhaps even his or her entire life. Let's use our words to build others up, not tear them down. An edifice is an impressively large building. No matter how imposing a skyscraper seems, however, it started out the same as smaller buildings and was built brick by brick. Let's edify one another. Let's build one another up—just like large, imposing buildings—brick by brick. Let's help others see that God has given them skyscraper potential. Kind words bring life, but cruel words can crush one's spirit.

Who are you going to edify today?

Holy Spirit Power

At that time the Spirit of the Lord will come powerfully upon you, and you will prophesy with them. You will be changed into a different person. (1 Sam. 10:6 NLT)

Prior to Jesus's birth, God's Spirit fell powerfully on individuals. Saul, in this verse, was prophesized to transform into a different person and receive a new heart when the Spirit of the Lord came upon him. Because of Jesus's life, death, and resurrection, God's Spirit comes upon us when we accept Him as our Lord and Savior. The same Spirit that changed Saul and gave him a new heart now permanently lives inside us. Our bodies have become temples of God's Spirit. Our salvation—our change from who we were to who we are since accepting God—is just as miraculous as Saul's. Like Saul's heart our hearts also have been changed. If previous sins, mistakes, and wrong choices have prevented you from getting closer to God or becoming active in church, remind the condemner, Satan, that you're changed and filled with the Spirit of God. His power is in you to help you do what you couldn't do before.

What do you need the power of the Spirit of God to help you do today?

_____

_____

_____

_____

You Are Able

Saul replied, "But I'm only from the tribe of Benjamin, the smallest tribe in Israel, and my family is the least important of all the families of that tribe! Why are you talking like this to me?" (1 Sam. 9:21 NLT)

Have you ever felt inadequate, unqualified, and insecure when you know God is pushing you toward a certain goal? God wanted Saul to lead Israel, but Saul had a million excuses as to why he wasn't the best candidate for the job. Whatever comes your way; you're equipped to handle with excellence! When work overwhelms you, you can do it. When kids, family, and finances seem unmanageable, you're able to handle it. When the enemy, Satan, whispers in your ear that you will fail, then you know you can do it! He is a liar and cannot tell the truth, so the opposite of what he's telling you is true. No matter what comes your way, you will be able to do it because God is with you.

What dream have you put on hold because you felt inadequate? Take a moment to write down your dreams, plans, and hopes for your future.

The God of the Impossible

*"There's a young boy here with five barley loaves and two fish.
But what good is that with this huge crowd?"(John 6:9 NLT)*

How strong is your faith? In this verse Andrew didn't believe that five loaves of bread and two fish could feed five thousand men, women, and children. He'd forgotten that with God all things are possible to those who believe. Your budget may look as if you don't have enough to make ends meet. Your marriage may seem as if it's headed for divorce. Your body may feel as if it never will be healed. But remember God! With God one plus one can be whatever it needs to be. Use your "faith eyes" instead of your natural eyes because God is able to do more than we can ask or think. Never underestimate His miraculous power. He is the same yesterday, today, and forever, so if He performed a miracle by feeding five thousand people with five loaves and two fish, He will perform miracles for you. How strong is your faith?

What is one thing you are willing to trust God to miraculously accomplish in your life?

Gratitude

Who can list the glorious miracles of the Lord? Who can ever praise him enough? (Ps. 106:2 NLT)

Sometimes life is so hectic that we forget to take the time to appreciate the world in which we live as well as the God who made it for us. Praise Him for green trees, blue skies, blue oceans, and the eyes to see it all. Praise Him for the sounds of birds chirping, children laughing, beautiful music, and the ears that enable us to hear. Praise Him for family, friends, children, mothers, fathers, and people who love you. Praise Him for the roof over your head and food to eat and all the comforts in your home. Never take all you have for granted. Tomorrow isn't guaranteed. Who can ever praise God enough?

What are you grateful to God for today?

Take Action

"I can't, sir," the sick man said, "for I have no one to put me into the pool when the water bubbles up. Someone else always gets there ahead of me." (John 5:7 NLT)

This man had been sick for thirty-eight years and would lie in front of the healing water, waiting for someone to help him in. Faith takes action. How many things have we put up with for years? We wait for someone to pray for us, to help us, to carry us to a place of healing—healing not only of our physical bodies but also of our emotions, our hurts, our guilt, our unforgiveness, our bitterness, our low self-esteem, and sometimes our hatred of others or ourselves. Today take action. Get up and receive your healing. Jesus already paid the price.

What steps will you take today to demonstrate your faith?

If He Says It, Believe It!

Then Jesus told him, "Go back home. Your son will live!" And the man believed what Jesus said and started home. (John 4:50 NLT)

This man, whose son was dying, took Jesus at His word. He didn't need Jesus to accompany him home or touch his son; he needed Him only to say the word. No "what ifs" entered his mind. He walked by faith, not sight. We must learn from this man. Fear and faith cannot coexist. Take Jesus at His word. If He said that all things are possible to those who believe, then you can do it. If He says that all your needs are met according to His riches in glory, then they are. If He says there's a plan and purpose for your life, then there is. Cast out fear and believe God at His word. If He said it, then that settles it!

What word has God put on your heart regarding your situation?

Never Be Thirsty

"But those who drink the water I give will never be thirsty again. It becomes a fresh, bubbling spring within them, giving them eternal life." (John 4:14 NLT)

I s there a void in your life? Have you allowed life's problems to make you lose your joy? The cares of this world can be heavy burdens, but you're not supposed to be carrying them—you're supposed to have handed them to Jesus. You're supposed to be full of the living water that Jesus gives so you'll never be thirsty again. Fill the void with more of Him and get your joy back. Play praise music, and sing and dance before Him until your joy returns. You may not feel like doing this, but that's why it's called the sacrifice of praise. Get into God's word, and ask Him to make it come alive to you. Spend quiet time in His presence, listening to what He speaks in your heart. Drink every day of His goodness, and never thirst again.

When is the last time you danced before the Lord?

We Are a Work in Progress

For God is working in you, giving you the desire and the power to do what pleases him. (Phil. 2:13 NLT)

God is working in you, and slowly but surely, He is changing your desires. With His help we can overcome things that once controlled us. We can say no to addictions, unforgiveness, fornication, and hatred when before we could not. Sometimes we fail not just once but many times. The only man who walked this earth and didn't sin was Jesus. We must remember that God is continuously working in us. It may seem like a slow process, but bit by bit, the fruit of the Spirit is being developed in each and every one of our lives. Love, peace, joy, and patience may not be evident the way you hope today. Perhaps your fruit is a bud or still green, but trust God. Perhaps your desires haven't changed yet, and you still fall to sin, but if you truly want to change, God will help you. God's grace enables us to do what we aren't able to do by ourselves.

Can you think of something that you used to do, contrary to God's will, which you no longer desire to do?

_____

_____

_____

_____

_____

_____

_____

No Condemnation

He forgives all my sins and heals all my diseases. (Ps. 103:3 NLT)

No matter how awful you feel your sin was, God has forgiven you. The word says that *all* your sins are forgiven. If you still feel guilty or condemned about something in your past, it's a lie from the Devil. God's word already has told you the truth, and there is no condemnation for those in Christ Jesus. You are reborn—born again—as a new creature in Christ. Remind yourself of this every time the thought crosses your mind of that sin committed by that totally different person who didn't know Christ. If you've missed the mark as your new creation, confess, repent, and forget the sin, just as Christ does. It's under the blood, meaning already paid for by Jesus shed blood on the cross. You don't have to continue to have guilt because your debt has been paid.

Can you think of any area of your life where the enemy constantly tries to condemn you?

Never Forget

Let all that I am praise the Lord; may I never forget the good things he does for me. (Ps. 103:2 NLT)

Usually we pray for something and beg God for what seems to be the most important thing in our lives. For about a week or two, we're ecstatic when God answers, then happy for a week or two, until our next prayer request comes. Then we wonder whether He will answer *this* prayer. What if He doesn't? What if...? Sounds a lot like the children of Israel, who forgot their deliverance from bondage, their protection from the plagues and the death angel, as well as the parting of the Red Sea. Keep a prayer journal. Write down your prayer and date it. Then write down your answered prayer and your feelings at that time and date that entry as well. Read your journal every day so you won't forget all the good things God has done for you.

Take a moment to write down every blessing God has given you.

Trust God

This I declare about the Lord: He alone is my refuge, my place of safety; he is my God, and I trust him. (Ps. 91:2 NLT)

When you're worried, afraid, or confused, to whom do you turn? Whom do you trust more, your friends or God? You develop your relationship with God by spending time with Him in prayer and His word. The more time you spend with Him, the more intimate your relationship with Him will be. He will be your best friend, your confidant, and your refuge. He wants to be the one you run to first, the one with whom you feel safe and secure, and the one you trust. Take a few moments before you start your day, before you close your eyes at night, and whenever you can during today to talk to Him. Tell Him what's going on with you as well as your dreams, your concerns, and your prayers, and you'll see how quickly this practice becomes your norm. He's there waiting, and He cares for you.

Why can you believe that God is trustworthy?

Guard Yourself

I will refuse to look at anything vile and vulgar. I hate all who deal crookedly; I will have nothing to do with them. (Ps. 101:3 NLT)

What we see and hear as Christians is important to God. Movies, music, books, TV shows, and acquaintances—you must filter all of these. We have free will to make decisions, but it's incorrect to think these things won't affect you. We often don't think much about what we watch, hear, or read, but it's time to start. If Jesus lives in you, He's there when you're surrounded by dirty language, dirty jokes, dirty songs, sexually explicit movies, etc. Take a minute and filter what you allow yourself to be exposed to. Remember, God is with you always.

What have been some negative influences in your life? How can you start eliminating them today?

_____

_____

_____

_____

_____

_____

_____

_____

_____

_____

_____

Godly Friends

Stay away from fools, for you won't find knowledge on their lips.
(Prov. 14:7 NLT)

The company we keep is very important. People identify you by observing the people with whom you spend time. We always must avoid the appearance of evil, so watch where you are and whom you're with, even though it may be innocent. Unless you spend most of your time with faith-filled, faith-talking, faith-walking Christians, it will be difficult for you to live victoriously. Just because someone is your best friend and you've known him or her for many years doesn't mean he or she can offer you godly advice. The people close to you may offer advice based on emotions, books, and experiences, but you need friends and confidants who seek God on your behalf. Let's find godly friends, stay in church, and stay in the word, so we can live the abundant lives God has promised us.

Which of your friends helps you live a Godly lifestyle, and which make it more difficult?

_____

_____

_____

_____

_____

_____

_____

The Potter

But now, O Lord, you are our Father; we are the clay, and you are our potter; we are all the work of your hand. (Isa. 64:8 ESV)

We are the clay. What do you do with clay? You mold it and shape it into something beautiful and useful. Sometimes the clay becomes a vase, sometimes a coffee mug or a statue. As the potter you choose. The clay doesn't have the authority to tell us what it wants to do or be. Likewise we must be careful that we aren't telling our potter, the heavenly Father, what we want to do. Instead seek His will (which, by the way, will line up with your desire) because He knows us better than we know ourselves. Trust that whatever He chooses for us is good. Wherever He places us is the right place, and whenever He chooses to fulfill His word is the right timing. He's got this and doesn't need our help.

What do you feel God's purpose and plan is for your life?

_____

_____

_____

_____

_____

_____

_____

_____

_____

Be Set Free

Let the sea and everything in it shout his praise! Let the earth and all living things join in. (Ps. 98:7 NLT)

Praising God isn't the coolest or most popular thing to do in the twenty-first century. It probably won't help you get friends or make good impressions with strangers. Then what's the point in praising God? Well, it sets you free, humbles you, and lifts heavy burdens from your shoulders and gives them to God. It releases you to cast your cares onto Him. God wasn't embarrassed when He hung naked on a cross and was severely beaten for us. So we shouldn't be embarrassed to praise Him openly for all He's done in our lives.

What prevents you from praising God?

No More Excuses

"But Lord," Gideon replied, "how can I rescue Israel? My clan is the weakest in the whole tribe of Manasseh, and I am the least in my entire family!" (Judg. 6:15 NLT)

Have you ever given God excuses when you know He's put it in your heart to do something? You may think, *I can't tell them about you, Lord; they'll think I'm a fanatic* or *I can't apply for that job; I'm not qualified* or *I can't go back to school; I don't have the time or money.* When God places a desire in your heart, He will make a way out of no way. He will open doors no person can open and close doors no person can close for *you*! You must take a step blindly, not knowing where God is leading you. Doing this can be scary, but trust me, if you fall, He'll be there to pick you up. We walk by faith, not by sight. Trust God, and accomplish His plan and purpose for you.

Can you identify things, which you now know were excuses, which have kept you from totally fulfilling God's plan and purpose for you?

Priorities

And they forsook the Lord God of their fathers, who had brought them out of the land of Egypt; and they followed other gods from among the gods of the people who were all around them, and they bowed down to them; and they provoked the Lord to anger. (Judg. 2:12 NKJV)

Has God ever done anything for you? He brought the Israelites out of the bondage of Egypt, yet some of them served other gods. Which other things in your life have you made a god out of? Do you worship your children? Your job? Your workouts? Your family? Food? Money? Sleep? It's wrong to make anything a priority above God. Do you go to the gym before you pray or read God's word? Do you sleep late while professing not to have time to open your heart to His word? Do you work extra hours, forgetting who gave you the ability or the job? Let's not provoke God to anger, as some of the Israelites did. Let's make a conscious effort to make Him our only God every day.

What changes in your schedule will you purpose to make right now to demonstrate that God's your number one priority?

Humility

All these things my hand has made, and so all these things came to be, declares the Lord. But this is the one to whom I will look: he who is humble and contrite in spirit and trembles at my word. (Isa. 66:2 ESV)

Humility and obedience are what God wants of us. We all want Him to look our way, but often we want it to happen our way and not His way. To consider others better than you and to obey the word of God is His way. I'm not implying this is easy by any means, only that it's necessary for us to please God. Pride causes us to be unforgiving, to be easily offended, and to be unable to admit our shortcomings. With pride everything revolves around you, and you don't even see it. Ask God today to show you when pride raises its ugly head in you. This is one step we all can take to be obedient to the word of God.

Can you identify opportunities that God has placed in your path where you could show more humility?

He is the Restorer

And the Lord restored the fortunes of Job, when he had prayed for his friends. And the Lord gave Job twice as much as he had before. (Job 42:10 ESV)

Perhaps life dealt you some hard blows, and one wrong decision snowballed into a lot of misery. The words of the Bible still hold true: all things work together for good for those who love the Lord. Job suffered some hard blows too but only because God allowed Satan to attack him. Nothing will come your way that you can't handle. God allows what we experience for our own good, even though it may not seem good at the time. After Job's trial God restored to him twice as much as he had before. God is not a respecter of persons, so if He restored to Job, He will restore anything the Devil has stolen back to you! Has the Devil stolen your joy? Your health? Your marriage? Your children? Your finances? Your peace? God is the restorer yesterday, today, and forever.

What are you believing God to restore to you?

The Great I AM

Before the mountains were brought forth, or ever you had formed the earth and the world, from everlasting to everlasting you are God. (Ps. 90:2 ESV)

God is the alpha and omega, the beginning and end. He existed before anything else existed, and He is the creator of all. Remembering His power and omnipotence sometimes helps put our problems and trials into perspective. There isn't—and never will be—anything too difficult for Him. When God told Moses to tell Pharaoh to let His people go, Moses asked, "Who should I say sent me?" God replied, "Tell them I AM sent you." When you're tempted to worry today, remember whom you serve. You don't operate in your own power but the power of the great I AM. He lives in you!

Don't worry today! Write this verse down and pull it out when you start to feel overwhelmed and read it over and over again. Exodus 14:14 NLT The Lord himself will fight for you. Just stay calm.

Your Words Matter

Let the words of my mouth and the meditation of my heart be acceptable in Your sight, O Lord, my strength and my Redeemer. (Ps. 19:14 NKJV)

Would God be pleased with what we say and think? Often we speak without even thinking, and those who don't do this have thoughts they know they wouldn't dare say. Today make a conscious effort to monitor your tongue and your thoughts. Whatever is pure, whatever is holy—meditate on today's verse or your favorite verse all day long. Let it sink into your heart until it's no longer an effort to remember or do. Our God, who redeemed us from the curse of the law, deserves no less. Pray as David did that you will please God today.

What is your favorite bible verse, and why?

_____

_____

_____

_____

_____

_____

_____

_____

_____

_____

_____

You Can!

For by You I can run against a troop. By my God I can leap over a wall. (Ps. 18:29 NKJV)

You can! You can do whatever is necessary because you are in Christ Jesus. Some goals may seem unreachable, some victories unattainable, some tasks insurmountable, but you can truly do all things through Him. God can do more than we can imagine. Don't be convinced by the enormity of the task or goal. Instead be convinced because of the enormity of God. You can!

In your wildest imagination how do you envision your future? God can do more than even this seemingly unreachable desire.

Jesus Paid A High Price For You

Praise be to the God and Father of our Lord Jesus Christ! In his great mercy he has given us new birth into a living hope through the resurrection of Jesus Christ from the dead. (1 Pet. 1:3 NIV)

Remember that you have been given this life because of Jesus. You have been born again to serve Him. We have hope because not even death was too big for our God. Know that He is with you always. The omnipotent, omniscient, omnipresent, loving, powerful, faithful, King of Kings and Lord of Lords died for you and loves you. He was beaten, kicked, ridiculed, and lied about, but He stayed on that cross and died for us. But...He rose again. He lives not only seated at the right hand of God but also in our hearts. Thank you, Lord, for your great sacrifice. Thank you for conquering death and saving us from eternal separation from you. Thank you for salvation and abundance, just as you promised us.

How does it make you feel to know that your heavenly father endured so much on the cross just for you?

Listen to God

And those who know Your name will put their trust in You; For You, Lord, have not forsaken those who seek You. (Ps. 9:10 NKJV)

Trust God. When things aren't going the way you'd hoped, when you need direction, when you need advice, even when everything is perfect, trust God. Seek Him by praying and by studying His word. Have alone time with God. "Alone time" actually means you must stop talking, begging, and crying and just listen to God. Listen to His plan, and stop asking Him to bless your plan. He knows your beginning and end, so He's able to make decisions regarding your life that you know nothing about. He's there. Jesus is seated at the right hand of God, interceding for you right now. Trust Him because you serve a faithful God; a mighty God; an awesome, all-powerful, all-knowing God who loves you. He always has your back, but do you have His?

When was the last time that you actually were quiet before God, just listening to him?

Forgive Yourself

What is man that you are mindful of him, and the son of man that You visit him? (Ps. 8:4 NKJV)

I t's almost incomprehensible that the almighty God, creator of the universe, cares for us. Whether or not you can wrap your mind around this concept, He cares. As vast as the universe is, He has a wonderful plan of redemption in place for us so we can be brought back into fellowship with Him. Realizing that He would send His son to die as the ultimate sacrifice for our sins seems unfathomable. Everyday remember the price Jesus paid for you, but more importantly, remember why He paid this price. He died so you could live, because Jesus loves you. He loves you when others may think you're unlovable, when you do the wrong things, and when the fruit of the Spirit isn't really showing in your life. He forgives. He teaches. He guides. He forgets confessed sin. He loves you.

When do you feel most loved and when do you feel least loved by God? Remember His love for you never changes. Is it time for you to forgive yourself?

He who says he abides in Him ought himself also to walk just as He walked. (1 John 2:6 NKJV)

O uch! This is one of those verses that's easier to pass right over than to follow. We who call ourselves Christians actually should strive to live our lives imitating Jesus. This means walking in love, considering others to be greater than us, ministering to the sick and the lost, and trying to tell others about Him. Christ never walked in unforgiveness or had outbursts of anger, selfishness, envy, or strife. Follow His example. Think before you speak and act. Remember when the "WWJD" bracelets were so popular? Although they are not seen frequently now every Christian should still ask themselves that question several times a day. Children of the King should act like their Father.

As you face decisions today ask yourself, what would Jesus do?

We Have Everything We Need

Seeing that His divine power has granted to us everything pertaining to life and godliness, through the true knowledge of Him who called us by His own glory and excellence. (2 Pet. 1:3 NASB)

If you were a parent who had to leave your children for an extended amount of time, you would prepare before you left. You would think about where they would stay, and you'd leave money to provide for their every need. Likewise our heavenly Father has lovingly thought about us. He's already left us everything we need to live godly lives. The Holy Spirit dwells in us, guiding us and giving us power. Whenever we need to talk to God, we have access to Him through prayer 24/7. We have authority over the enemy as well as the armor to stand victoriously against his attacks. We have health, a sound mind, and abundance. Claim your inheritance today!

Have you been using everything that God has left here on earth for your benefit? Learn what you're entitled to receive as His child.

God is Not Limited by Time

But, beloved, do not forget this one thing, that with the Lord one day is as a thousand years, and a thousand years as one day.
(2 Pet. 3:8 NKJV)

Many of us have been diligently praying for things but have yet to see them come to pass. Remember, God's timing is not our timing. He isn't bound by time as we are. He knows the entire picture, while we see only a part. We must trust that no matter how things look at the moment, they're working out for our good. At this time in your life, you may not be able to handle the things you pray to God for. That loved one you want saved now may bring others to Christ if he or she is saved next year. The job you think you want may bring you more heartbreak than you realize. Trust God. He loves you and guides your every step. Again remember that His timing is not our timing.

Write the date and time when you begin praying for each need in your life down for your remembrance. Expect to check off each one of your requests in God's timing.

Humility

Therefore humble yourselves under the mighty hand of God, that He may exalt you in due time. (1 Pet. 5:6 NKJV)

Merriam-Webster Online Dictionary defines "humility" as "the quality or state of not thinking you are better than other people. "In today's society, people seek education, wealth, and experience. Nothing is inherently wrong with any of these things. However, when you begin to think you deserve more because of your status, when you look to other people for accolades because of who you think you are and all you've done, you're operating in pride instead of humility. Promotion, honor, and recognition come from God, not man. God sees your works when no one else does, and in *due* time He will exalt you. God is not man and does not lie—if He says it, it will happen! Therefore remain humble and wait for God.

What are some ways you can keep yourself from becoming prideful?

God Has Given You Gifts

As each one has received a gift, minister it to one another, as good stewards of the manifold grace of God. (1 Pet. 4:10 NKJV)

What is your God-given gift? Your gift may be organizational skills, crafts, cooking, children, writing, hospitality, exhortation, business, sports, gardening, or even giving. Think about what God has put in you that you could use to bless His people today. We are to be good stewards of His grace, love, and blessings. We must all take time out from "me," "mine," and "ours." It's time to seek His kingdom first and foremost in your life. Then and only then will all your desires be met.

What do you enjoy doing? How can you use this God given gift to glorify your King?

_____

_____

_____

_____

_____

_____

_____

_____

_____

_____

Why Me?

Beloved, do not think it strange concerning the fiery trial which is to try you, as though some strange thing happened to you.
(1 Pet. 4:12 NKJV)

"Why me?" This shouldn't be a question we ask when trials arise in our lives. It's not personal, and you've been forewarned. The question should be "How can I get through this trial victoriously?" Keeping God's word not just in your mind but also in your heart is the answer. Know that God is with you, and He is bigger than any trial. Doing these things means spending time praying to God, reading His word, and meditating on His promises until they're not just words but reality in your heart. Sometimes you'll have to remind yourself several times a day of God's promises. Walk around with a particular verse written on paper, and when you start to stress out, take it out and read it. Repeat the following as often as possible: "My God *shall* supply all my needs. I *can* do all things through Christ. By His stripes I *was* healed." Choose a promise, and stand on it today!

> **What is foremost in your list of prayers right now? Turn to your concordance in the back of your bible (or use the internet) to find scriptures relating to your concern. Now say it all day long and watch God honor His word.**

Entitled!

Having been justified by His grace we should become heirs according to the hope of eternal life. (Titus 3:7 NKJV)

We are justified. This means we became new creatures in Christ when we accepted Jesus. It's just as if we never sinned. Many times the enemy, trying to get us into condemnation, will remind us of every sin we've ever done. Remember that you are justified. Now, when we fall short, we must confess our sins to God, and He will forgive us. We are heirs, meaning we have been adopted by God and are entitled to all His blessings. *Entitled*! You are worthy of being blessed because His grace has cleansed you. If you're battling for something the Bible says you should have, stand boldly on the word until what you want is yours, because you're an heir and you're justified. Live this life abundantly, taking back everything the Devil has tried to keep from you today.

Renew your mind today to the fact that God sees you just as if you've never sinned.

Remember (Rom. 10:17 NKJV) So then faith comes by hearing, and hearing by the word of God.

Finish the Race

I have fought the good fight, I have finished the race, I have kept the faith. (2 Tim. 4:7 NKJV)

When it's time for you to stand before God, can you say these words that Paul spoke to Timothy? "I have fought the good fight, finished the race, and kept the faith." It's a good fight because it's one we can win! Life isn't a sprint but a marathon that requires endurance. To continue we must keep our eyes on the finish line. When we focus on the cares of this world, we lose our focus and fall behind or stop in our tracks. Every time you feel as if life is too much, remember that you've taken your eyes off God and are focusing on the problem. Sometimes you don't know where to put your next step, but you must not lose your faith. Trust God. He'll guide you one step at a time.

What are some practical steps you can start doing today to prepare yourself for this marathon called 'life' as a Christian?

Be Ready!

Preach the word! Be ready in season and out of season. Convince, rebuke, exhort, with all longsuffering and teaching. (2 Tim. 4:2 NKJV)

This verse sounds intimidating. Many of us think, *I don't know enough of the word to preach to anyone. I'm not that holy. Who am I to do that? Surely this verse was written for pastors and people who are social butterflies and don't have a problem speaking in public.* The Bible, however, was written for believers, and that includes each and every one of us. Preaching is telling about Jesus. It can be as easy as blessing your food in mixed company, leaving the room when people are telling dirty jokes, or sharing what God has done for you. To preach you don't have to know a single verse of the Bible! What can anyone one say when you share that God healed you, delivered you from addictions, helped you get a better job, or given you back your joy? Ask God to provide you with opportunity, and be ready at all times to share your experiences with others. Preach the word!

If someone asks you why you are a Christian are you prepared to tell your experience? What will you say?

_____

_____

_____

_____

_____

_____

Be the Bigger Person

But avoid foolish and ignorant disputes, knowing that they generate strife. (2 Tim. 2:23 NKJV)

A seemingly insignificant conversation sometimes can lead to the most volatile fights. When you look back at the situation, you may realize you never saw what was coming. You should have just kept quiet, and the tempers wouldn't have escalated. Pride, however, keeps us trying to prove our point and makes us not want to back down. Pride makes us feel our answer is the only right one. Many times we are absolutely right, but someone must back down or the relationship will suffer. Be the bigger person; let the love of God rule your heart. Your relationships with people are more important than being right or proving your point every time. God is love—let His love shine through you every day. He sees you. He knows your sacrifices. He won't forget your obedience. Do everything as if you were doing it unto God.

Why do you believe it is difficult for you to back down? Is it possible to change "the way you've always been"?

Don't Compromise

Yes, and all who desire to live godly in Christ Jesus will suffer persecution. (2 Tim. 3:12 NKJV)

We all desire to live carefree, happy, healthy, abundant, prosperous lives. The Bible, however, says if you desire to live a godly life, you will suffer persecution. People like people who fit in with the crowd; Christians should not. (John 17:14) I have given them your word, and the world has hated them because they are not of the world, just as I am not of the world. Our opinions of marriage, sex, and money do not conform to the majority of societies beliefs most of the time. This shouldn't be frightening because we won't be alone in whatever we face. God lives in us and never will leave us. Although Jesus was persecuted, He conquered death and rose again. God never will give you more than you can handle. When trials come your way, tell yourself, *God already has approved this; therefore I can do all things through Christ, who gives me strength.* All things work together for good for those who love the Lord. Everything will be OK because God is on your side!

Can you think of a time when your Christian opinion was unpopular, but you were glad that you didn't compromise?

Studying Pays Off

Be diligent to present yourself approved to God, a worker who does not need to be ashamed, rightly dividing the word of truth. (2 Tim. 2:15 NKJV)

We should do everything with Christ in mind. Our jobs, our homes, our marriages, and our relationships must be done with excellence so that God approves. When you stand before God, you don't want to be ashamed of having displayed a poor attitude, bad temper, or unforgiveness or causing others to stumble. Learn the word daily, so when you need it, you can use it not only in your own life but also to bless others. Rightly follow the word of truth, regardless of how you feel or how circumstances look. The truth is that you are an overcomer; you are blessed; you experience victory in every trial; you were healed two thousand years ago by the stripes on Jesus's back. All your needs are met according to His riches in glory!

How do you personally study the word of God during your private time with him? If you haven't been studying God's word, come up with a plan today to learn the word of God.

_____

_____

_____

_____

_____

We Are Soldiers

You therefore must endure hardship as a good soldier of Jesus Christ. (2 Tim. 2:3 NKJV)

We are in the army of the Lord. Even though we must fight the enemy, we don't need to be afraid. We have weapons that will pull down the strongholds in our lives. Have you ever had a problem, but no matter how hard you tried, you couldn't seem to get rid of it? Angry outbursts, cigarettes, alcohol, pride, substance abuse, gambling, fornication, and adultery are all strongholds. If you catch yourself thinking, *That's just me and my problem*, stop it! As a soldier use your weapons to pull these strongholds down and eliminate them from your life once and for all. There will be hardships in this life, but we can be victorious through Christ.

As a good soldier you must hold your standards high, be courageous, be loyal to God and fulfill your obligations. Can you truthfully say you are a good soldier in God's army?

I am Not Ashamed!

For this reason I also suffer these things; nevertheless I am not ashamed, for I know whom I have believed and am persuaded that He is able to keep what I have committed to Him until that day. (2 Tim. 1:12 NKJV)

Here Paul told Timothy that he was confident in who he was. He trusted God, and equally important, he was persuaded that God trusted him to do His will. Can you say the same? Are you confident in who you are in Christ? Do you trust Him to have your back on this journey called life? Can God trust you to be obedient to His will and His word? Will you stand boldly for what is right, regardless of what others say? Can God count on you to be His hands, eyes, and ears on earth, shining a light in the darkness? As you start this day and every day, make this your goal. Trust God. Be a light. Be a blessing. Make your heavenly Father proud.

What can you do to make your heavenly Father proud today?

God's Grace

Share with me in the sufferings for the gospel according to the power of God, who has saved us and called us with a holy calling, not according to our works, but according to His own purpose and grace which was given to us in Christ Jesus before time began. (2 Tim. 1:8–9 NKJV)

Before the beginning of time, God had a plan for us: to bring humankind, separated from Him because of sin, back into fellowship with Him. Because of God's grace, Jesus paid the ultimate price for us, and now we are back in fellowship, standing with God, righteous. Your life was paid for with such a heavy price that you must no longer live for yourself but for God. Ask Him which path to take today, how to be a blessing, which friends to be in fellowship with, which places you need to be. Be bold in witnessing as you remember the price Jesus paid for you. His grace is sufficient for all you need today. He saved you and called you with a holy calling, not because of what you have done but because of His plan for you and His grace.

God's grace gives you the power to do what you need in every situation. As you go through your day remind yourself that it's available for you.

Therefore I remind you to stir up the gift of God, which is in you through the laying on of my hands. (2 Tim. 1:6 NKJV)

There is a God-given plan and purpose for each of our lives. It's unique, specially designed just for you. He knew you before you were in your mother's womb. He knows the number of hairs on your head. He lives in you as the Holy Spirit, guiding you daily. He sits on the right side of God, interceding on your behalf daily as Jesus. He, the Father, loves you so much that He sent Jesus, His only son, to die for you. Never doubt that you're special. Never feel inadequate or unloved or incapable of accomplishing whatever God has put in your heart to do. You have gifts and talents that no one else has. Never forget how special you are and the unique calling of God in your life!

What is it that you are doing when you totally lose track of time? Ask your best friend or family members what your talents and gifts are today.

It's A Good Fight

Fight the good fight of the faith. Take hold of the eternal life to which you were called and about which you made the good confession in the presence of many witnesses. (1 Tim. 6:12 ESV)

We have publicly acknowledged Christ and are now in a battle with the enemy. Your main defensive weapon is your breastplate of righteousness. Everything you did before you accepted Christ is forgotten in his eyes, removed as far as the east is from the west. You are the righteousness of God, not because of your own goodness but because of what Jesus suffered for you on the cross. You can stand boldly before the Devil and not in condemnation of any sin he tries to bring to your remembrance. Your main offensive weapon is the sword of the Spirit, which is the word of God. Read it; memorize it; learn it; and use it. Fight every attack of the enemy with your arsenal. Why is it a good fight of faith? Because if we believe in Him, we win!

Did you know that your righteousness is not based on how you feel? Convince yourself of this fact today.

_____

_____

_____

_____

_____

_____

_____

Secret to Being Rich

For the love of money is a root of all kinds of evils. It is through this craving that some have wandered away from the faith and pierced themselves with many pangs. (1 Tim. 6:10 ESV)

God wants us to be prosperous and have abundant lives. Prosperity doesn't include just money but also happy homes, good reputations, loving marriages, health, children, and families that serve God. The path to true prosperity isn't through get-rich-quick schemes but by seeking Him first. The word says He will supply all our needs according to His riches in glory. Concentrate on developing your relationship with God, hearing His voice, loving people, and accepting His guidance in everything you do. This is the secret to being rich!

Keeping in mind the true prosperity definition, are you rich?

Set Your Hope on God

For to this end we toil and strive, because we have our hope set on the living God, who is the Savior of all people, especially of those who believe. (1 Tim. 4:10 ESV)

Are you "hoping" for prosperity, health, a stronger marriage, a better job, or the salvation of family members? Your hope should be set on your God, the King of Kings and Lord of Lords. Faith is the substance of things hoped for and the evidence of things not seen. Place your hope and faith in the one who is able to make it all come to pass. People—including your friends, your boss, and even your spouse—will let you down, but God won't! He is able to do more than we can imagine or think. He is bigger than all your problems. He is faithful. Have your hope set on the living God.

Has God been faithful to you?

Spiritually Fit

Have nothing to do with irreverent, silly myths. Rather train
yourself for godliness. (1 Tim. 4:7 ESV)

Watching the news, reading Facebook posts, and listening to friends shouldn't be how we make decisions in our lives unless their source is God's word. A lot of things sound legitimate at first but then are proven over time not to be trustworthy. God's word, however, is the same yesterday, today, and forever. Train yourself in godliness just as hard as you train your physical body when you work out. Get your sweat on, because if there's no pain, there's no gain physically or spiritually. Use God's word as your standard in all you do. It may not be easy, but in the end, you'll be spiritually fit, stronger in Christ, and completely ready to defeat the enemy.

Are you ready to start your spiritual workout? How will you begin to change your normal routine?

He'll Do It Again!

He who calls you is faithful; he will surely do it. (1 Thess. 5:24 ESV)

Is anything too difficult for God? We are amazed by the Israelites, who witnessed miracle after miracle and still doubted God's ability, but are we any better? How did you get to this point in your life? Do you think your own abilities are the reason, or might it be by the grace of God? How many of us have been in a car accident but are still alive and well? How many of us have fallen asleep at the wheel but are still here? Have you ever been in a potentially dangerous situation, but by the grace of God, no harm came to you? This same God, who has protected you your whole life, is the one who *will* answer your prayers. He is faithful. He has come to your aid in the past. Just remember, He'll do it again!

Think of a time when God has come to your aid in the past and use this memory to build your faith for your future.

Accountability

We exhorted each one of you and encouraged you and charged you to walk in a manner worthy of God, who calls you into his own kingdom and glory. (1 Thess. 2:12 ESV)

We must encourage one another in the Lord. Everyone does better when they're held accountable. If you try to lose weight alone, it's usually hard. In contrast if you know you have to weigh yourself in front of someone else, you may think twice before reaching for dessert. Being held accountable makes you think twice. We must walk in a worthy manner. Let's study the word together, participate in fellowship together, and build one another up so we can all walk in a manner that is worthy of God. Let's think twice before disobeying His word. Let's think twice before we let our flesh rule us. Together we can do this!

Do you have someone in your life that will hold you accountable?

Seasoned Speech

Let your speech always be gracious, seasoned with salt, so that you may know how you ought to answer each person. (Col. 4:6 ESV)

Sometimes we must wait before we speak. The tongue is powerful. Before we say what we think, or give anyone a piece of our minds, we must season our speech. Salt adds flavor and preserves. Does what you're about to say help the situation, edify someone, or tear down and destroy? Remember, once you release your words, you can't take them back. Let's take a minute and train ourselves so that our speech will be gracious. That action alone provides a powerful example to others and serves God. With the Holy Spirit helping you, this is doable. Show everyone how powerful your God is by seasoning your speech.

Take a minute before you speak today and make sure what you're about to say is properly seasoned.

Peace

And let the peace of Christ rule in your hearts, to which indeed you were called in one body. And be thankful. (Col. 3:15 ESV)

Do you allow the peace of Christ to rule in your heart? God's peace doesn't always make sense. It comes in the midst of a trial, when you should be screaming and crying, yet you keep on keeping on, knowing everything will be OK. God's peace is always available to all believers, but you must surrender the issue to God. As long as you think, *I've got this;* you'll worry and have sleepless nights. Cast all your cares on Him, and enjoy God's peace. Then thank Him for loving you and caring enough about you to take your test and turn it into your testimony.

> When you've been studying the word and spending time with God you will have peace in the worst circumstances. Start studying today with this verse Psalm 119:165 NIV, Great peace have those who love your law, and nothing can make them stumble.

Yearn for More

My soul waits for the Lord more than watchmen for the morning,
more than watchmen for the morning. (Ps. 130:6 ESV)

Watchmen stay up all night, protecting others from danger. When their shifts are almost over, they're tired and count down the minutes until they can get in bed. Have you ever been driving and been so sleepy that all you could think about was getting home? Other drivers might even have honked their horns as you dozed at red lights. You should wait for God even more than you yearn for your bed after a lack of sleep. You should long for Him and be excited about spending time alone with Him. You should be excited as you read God's word and He makes it come alive to you. If you're not there yet, start by asking God to energize your desire to be in fellowship with Him. He will if you first make the time.

When you first accepted Christ you were probably excited about the word. As you live life this excitement waxes and wanes. What can you do to reignite your fire and passion for Christ?

_____

_____

_____

_____

_____

_____

_____

Imitate Good

Beloved, do not imitate evil but imitate good. Whoever does good is from God; whoever does evil has not seen God. (3 John 1:11 ESV)

We must be leaders, not followers. Whom we choose to spend our time with is important. Sometimes we're with our old friends and want to do what they're doing, even though we're new creatures in Christ. We must, however, get to the point where what God thinks—and our obedience to God—is more important to us than what our friends (or family members) think about us. Find someone you look up to who follows the Lord and imitate him or her. The apostle Paul says, "Follow me as I follow Christ."

Who is your spiritual mentor? If you do not have one, who do you look up to?

Take Action!

For we walk by faith, not by sight. (2 Cor. 5:7 NKJV)

How do we get the faith to believe in God's promises despite what we see? We must hear the word over and over. We must go to church more than once a week. We must attend Bible studies and spend personal time with God. He will help you understand the word more and more if you ask Him to. It's time to stop realizing that it's important to study the word—*it's time to do it*! Use your Facebook time, Instagram time, lunchtime, movie time, and your sleep time. Use whatever it takes to hear the word so you can walk by faith, not sight.

> **Ask God today to help you organize your schedule to make time for more of Him. What things truthfully occupy the majority of your time?**

You were Chosen

*But you are a chosen race, a royal priesthood, a holy nation,
a people for his own possession, that you may proclaim the
excellencies of him who called you out of darkness into his
marvelous light. (1 Pet. 2:9 ESV)*

Remember that God chose you. Every time the enemy tries to remind you of your past or your failures, remember that you were chosen by God, set apart, for a specific plan and purpose. You are His special possession, and you are loved. When everyone else turns his or her back, doesn't understand, or lets you down, God still loves you. As you think of His goodness, His faithfulness, and His love, don't forget to give Him the praise He deserves.

What do you think God has in store for you personally?

Ready For Battle

We know that anyone born of God does not continue to sin; the one who was born of God keeps him safe, and the evil one cannot harm him.(1 John 5:18 NIV)

Sometimes we give the Devil too much credit. He already has been defeated, yet we make his lies in our heads louder than God's truths. We know we'll win in the end, but we're still afraid to fight him with the word of God. Yes, he's an enemy, which can be disheartening, but isn't it better knowing that you'll win every battle against him? Usually we don't know the outcome of the battles we are forced to fight. You know Satan is coming, and you even know he's bringing fiery darts to attack. So get dressed for battle with the armor God has given you. Are you ready for the battle? If not, get ready! Study, read, go to church, and spend time with the right people. The Devil can't touch you if you don't let him.

Is your armor polished and ready for the battle? If not, read Ephesians 6:10-18 and start to prepare yourself.

You Are Royalty

And if children, then heirs—heirs of God and fellow heirs with Christ, provided we suffer with him in order that we may also be glorified with him. (Rom. 8:17 ESV)

When you accepted Christ, you were adopted into the family, and He became your Father. He is the King of Kings and Lord of Lords, which makes you heir to His throne, royalty. "Ye are a chosen generation, a royal priesthood," states 1 Peter 2:9. Why don't we act as if our heavenly Father is powerful? Why don't we act like royalty? We must stop allowing the Devil to beat us up and put him under our feet, where he belongs. Remind him of who you are and who your Father is. Stand firm on the word of God, and don't allow the Devil to bully you ever again!

Has the devil been bullying you and causing your self-esteem to be less than it should be as a child of a King?

_____

_____

_____

_____

_____

_____

_____

_____

Eyes of Faith

We do not look at the things which are seen, but at the things which are not seen. For the things which are seen are temporary, but the things which are not seen are eternal. (2 Cor. 4:18 NKJV)

We must walk by faith, not by sight. What you see in the physical world may be discouraging, but stop looking at what you see with your eyes and start seeing the word by faith. Your bank account says your bills won't get paid this month, but God's word says God shall supply all your needs according to His riches in glory. Your body feels sick, but the word says you were healed two thousand years ago by the stripes Jesus took on His back. Keep your mind on the word and the eternal. The eternal is your obedience to Christ, your love for His people, and your daily interactions with Him. Learn to see with spiritual eyes instead of your physical eyes.

What circumstances are you facing at this time that you need to start looking at with eyes of faith?

_____

_____

_____

_____

_____

_____

_____

Daily Renewal

Therefore we do not lose heart. Even though our outward man is perishing, yet the inward man is being renewed day by day.
(2 Cor. 4:16 NKJV)

Our bodies aren't meant to last for eternity. We may do our best to keep them in the best physical shape we can, but they age and eventually die. Our inward man, however, never dies. To be absent from these bodies is to be with Christ. Every day, as the outer man ages, the inner man grows stronger and more powerful. The Devil no longer can trip you up as he did in the past, because you've grown in Christ. You know more of God's word; you've seen God act on your behalf more; and you've learned how to persevere. Your inner man is strong! You will continue to grow stronger each day as you live according to the word of God.

Are you in a different place spiritually than you were a year ago, or five years ago? The word of God is the key to your spiritual fountain of youth.

We are hard-pressed on every side, yet not crushed; we are perplexed, but not in despair; persecuted, but not forsaken; struck down, but not destroyed. (2 Cor. 4:8–9 NKJV)

Because of our faith in God, we are not crushed or in despair when all hell breaks loose. When you know whom you serve, you don't have to be perplexed or feel forsaken, regardless of what the situation looks like. Nothing should keep you down, because the Bible says a righteous man falls down seven times but gets back up. You will not be destroyed, regardless of what Satan tries. Keep your joy and peace as you go through trials, because you can be confident that this too will pass, and you will come out shining on the other side.

Is all hell breaking loose in your world right now? For His anger *is but for* a moment, His favor *is for* life; weeping may endure for a night, but joy *comes* in the morning. (*Ps. 30:5 NKJV*) How will you keep your joy?

_____

_____

_____

_____

_____

_____

_____

_____

_____

Be Steadfast

Therefore, my beloved brothers, be steadfast, immovable, always abounding in the work of the Lord, knowing that in the Lord your labor is not in vain. (1 Cor. 15:58 ESV)

In the Lord your labor is not in vain. Knowing this makes this Christian walk much easier. As you get up every day and go out into a world where you're considered peculiar and where you try to let your light shine but get little reward, remember that God sees. He knows when you wanted to curse someone out but stopped because you thought about your heavenly Father and made a choice for Christ. He knows when you extended kindness in the midst of a hectic day. So continue to be immovable and steadfast. Let nothing and no one steer you off your course for Jesus! God will reward you in due time.

What things, people, activities are threatening to steer you off your course for Jesus?

_____

_____

_____

_____

_____

_____

_____

_____

Love

Anyone who does not love does not know God, because God is love. (1 John 4:8 ESV)

Love is patient and kind, doesn't insist on its own way, and keeps no record of wrongs. If we aren't able to love, the Bible says we don't really know God. Put away any unforgiveness in your heart today. You don't have to keep the person you're at odds with in your inner circle, but don't wish him or her any harm. Work on perfecting your love walk. It's a command of God, and it's important!

Have you truly forgiven everyone who has hurt you, insulted you, belittled you or offended you? Ask God to enlarge your heart today to forgive them so that your prayers are not hindered. (Mark 11:26 NKJV)

Never Alone

Little children, you are from God and have overcome them, for he who is in you is greater than he who is in the world. (1 John 4:4 ESV)

The greater one lives in you. Your body is the temple of the Holy Spirit. God is always with you. You are an overcomer because you are filled with God. Whether or not you feel He's there doesn't matter because the word says He is. We're a people who should walk by according to what the word of God says, and not by what we see., God never will leave or forsake you. He's bigger than every problem, situation, and any drama life dishes out. So as you face today, remember that you have the greater one in you. You are fully able to handle whatever comes your way because you are not alone!

How can you adjust your schedule to talk to God throughout this day? This critical step will increase your faith to believe that God is with you always.

Strive for Holiness

If we confess our sins, he is faithful and just to forgive us our sins and to cleanse us from all unrighteousness. (1 John 1:9 ESV)

Making a mistake and living a lifestyle of sin are two different things. We all mess up. Sometimes we miss the mark every once in a while but other times we fall short several times in a day. Praise God for His grace, because now we can confess our sins to Him, and He not only forgives us but also makes it as if we've never done it to start with. A lifestyle of sin is one in which you plan to repeat the sin, often or daily, and don't feel sad or guilty about it. Let's not allow the enemy to condemn us for sins that we've already confessed before God and that we plan never to do again. Let us make our sins infrequent as we strive to be holy, as God is holy.

Love, joy, peace, forbearance, kindness, goodness, faithfulness, gentleness and self-control are the fruit of the Spirit. Which of these needs to grow in you as you strive to be holy?

Do nothing from selfish ambition or conceit, but in humility count others more significant than yourselves. (Phil. 2:3 ESV)

*L*ord, help me to be rich, you might pray. *Lord, help me to get a promotion.* Well, what's your motive? Do you want these things because of conceit or selfish ambition or to be a blessing God's people? Everything we do in this vapor called life isn't about accumulating "things" or "riches" that we can't take to the grave. It's about people—loving people, helping people, being a vessel God can use on this earth to be a blessing. We must give God the glory in everything we do. When we take on this mind-set, our happiness is about pleasing Christ, so our emotions are more stable. Our joy is permanent instead of dependent upon our circumstances. Check your motives every day. Allow your words, actions, and life to represent God well.

Do you think your words; actions and life represent God favorably?

Compassionate Hearts

Put on then, as God's chosen ones, holy and beloved,
compassionate hearts, kindness, humility, meekness, and
patience, bearing with one another and, if one has a complaint
against another, forgiving each other; as the Lord has forgiven
you, so you also must forgive. (Col. 3:12–13 ESV)

Forgiveness is a command and easier to talk about than actually do. Jesus forgave those who lied about Him, beat Him, spat on Him, and mocked Him. He said, "Father, forgive them, because they don't know what they're doing." He forgave us and adopted us into His family. He forgave all our sins and died for us, so shouldn't we try to forgive those who have hurt us? If you find yourself always angry or offended, it's probably because of pride. Pride makes you so caught up in yourself that you think everything done or said is about you. Unforgiveness stops our prayers in their tracks. The next time you find an opportunity to be angry or offended, don't go there. Forgive as Christ forgave you.

Why do you think forgiving others is so difficult?

Shield of Faith

In all circumstances take up the shield of faith, with which you can extinguish all the flaming darts of the evil one. (Eph. 6:16 ESV)

The Devil comes to steal, kill, and destroy. He sends fiery darts to try to disrupt your world. Examples of fiery darts include a stupid argument, a pay cut, car repairs, someone gossiping about you, marriage problems, or a death in family. Your faith is the shield you use for protection. When problems arise be aware that they're happening in your life, but choose to stand on His word. No weapon formed against you shall succeed. If God is for you, who can be against you? God hasn't given you a spirit of fear but rather love, power, and a sound mind. By His stripes you are healed. Your faith extinguishes every dart the Devil will try to throw your way, every time!

Find the verse to stop the fiery dart that Satan has been throwing at you right now.

_____

_____

_____

_____

_____

_____

_____

_____

Look for Opportunity

So then, as we have opportunity, let us do good to everyone, and especially to those who are of the household of faith. (Gal. 6:10 ESV)

Look for opportunity. If you don't look, you won't see the need. If you ask God every day for an opportunity for you to be a blessing, that opportunity will come. We often get caught up in life, problems, drama, and ourselves. We pray for help, for deliverance from the messes we've made, for help when we don't know what to do. We pray for ourselves, but when we take our prayers off ourselves and pray for others, help others, and do good for others, all our needs will be met. You can keep struggling, doing things your way, or do things God's way and have all your needs met. It's your choice to make today.

How can you make a God opportunity in your life so you can bless someone today?

_____

_____

_____

_____

_____

_____

_____

_____

God is Good

Ephesians 5:20 ESV

giving thanks always and for everything to God the Father in the name of our Lord Jesus Christ. (Eph. 5:20 ESV)

Today God has blessed me with another year of health, strength, and sound mind. I lost people I loved last year, which makes me realize even more how grateful I am for my husband, my children, and my friends. I thank God for being with me through the good times and the bad. I can testify to the fact that He is faithful. Today I'm reminded of all my blessings, but let's not remember His goodness only on special days but every day. When things aren't working out the way you'd like, God is still good. When you feel as though you can't handle the problems in your life and won't make it another day, God is still good. Whether the bills are paid or unpaid, God is still good. Whether you're feeling up or down, God is good. Thank you, Lord, for your faithfulness in the name of Jesus.

List a few reasons why you can truthfully say, "God is good to me".

Love Your Neighbor

For the whole law is fulfilled in one word: "You shall love your neighbor as yourself." (Gal. 5:14 ESV)

How many times a day do you think about others? When was the last time you went out of your way to perform a random act of kindness? How do we love ourselves? We encourage, feed, dress, and shelter ourselves every day. We never should condemn ourselves, but instead we should pray for ourselves and want the best for ourselves. Let's stretch and be obedient, and enlarge our world to include others. Most of the time, when we ask someone how he or she is doing, we don't really want to hear what that person has to say because we're too busy. Take a minute next time; make sure the person is encouraged, fed, and sheltered, and pray for him or her if necessary. Visit the sick and those in prison. Clothe and feed the homeless from time to time. It's a command from God. You take care of His people, and He will take care of you. You reap what you sow.

Think as people cross your path today, "If I were in this situation what would I want done for me"?

The Love Walk

For in Christ Jesus neither circumcision nor uncircumcision counts for anything, but only faith working through love. (Gal. 5:6 ESV)

Love is what it's all about—not whether you've performed some ritual or obeyed the religious custom of a church. If you're the holiest one in your denomination and do everything according to the book but don't know how to walk in love, you displease God. We must work on our love walk every day. Don't focus on just the people you love but also on those less fortunate. Love the family members who are easy to dislike. Treat people the way you'd like to be treated—the way they deserve to be treated as children of God. Be a light. Be the salt. Be a blessing. Walk in love as Jesus did.

The next big holiday that you'll be with family members who tend to rub you the wrong way; what can you do to show them the love of God?

The Blessing of Abraham

So that in Christ Jesus the blessing of Abraham might come to the Gentiles, so that we might receive the promised Spirit through faith. (Gal. 3:14 ESV)

By our faith we receive the blessing of Abraham. One of the first promises God made to Abraham appears in Genesis 12:2: "I will make of thee a great nation, and I will bless thee, and make thy name great; and thou shalt be a blessing: And I will bless them that bless thee, and curse him that curseth thee: and in thee shall all families of the earth be blessed." Receive the promise today! When you are attacked, speak the word! The promises God made to Abraham are yours. You're standing on God's word, which says God will bless those who bless Him and curse those who curse Him. Don't rely on other people to promote you, but trust God because His word says He will make your name great. You have the favor of God. Wake up every day expecting to be a blessing because God has said it is so.

Speak Abraham's blessing throughout the day until you believe it in your heart. Substitute your name in the verse (Genesis 12:2 above) every time it says thee or thou.

You're A New Creature

I have been crucified with Christ. It is no longer I who live, but Christ who lives in me. And the life I now live in the flesh I live by faith in the Son of God, who loved me and gave himself for me. (Gal. 2:20 ESV)

Let's follow Paul's example. The old you is dead, and you're a new creature in Christ! Don't allow Satan to condemn you for the poor life choices you made in the past. Live every day by faith. Trust God for direction, even regarding where to place your next footstep. Christ gave because He loves us—not like people love but with a love that never fails, a love that endures, a love that is patient. Christ doesn't rejoice in your wrongdoing but believes in you and is kind. Although He wants us to obey, He doesn't insist on His own way but gives us the freedom to choose. This magnificent, awesome, powerful God lives in you. He never will leave you or forsake you. So start off each day as Paul did, saying, "It is no longer I who live, but Christ who lives in me."

Who do people usually see when they are around you; the old you or the reborn you filled with Christ?

Hard Work

For we speak as messengers approved by God to be entrusted with the Good News. Our purpose is to please God, not people. He alone examines the motives of our hearts.
(1 Thess. 2:4 NLT)

Paul, Silas and Timothy are speaking to the church of Thessalonica in this verse. They were severely persecuted for trying to preach about Jesus. Christians still face persecution today. According to Open Doors USA Christians are the most persecuted religious group worldwide. An average of at least 180 Christians around the world are killed each month for their faith. Paul, Silas and Timothy still preached the good news of Jesus Christ with pure motives despite the fact they would suffer physical harm. The gospel of Jesus is no less important today than it was during their lives. Fortunately in the United States we can assemble, read our bibles and pray in public without fear of losing our lives, being imprisoned or hurt. We must not take our freedom lightly but use everything at our disposal to learn about our Lord. Pray for those Christians living in countries where there's persecution today. Thank God for your religious freedom and never take it for granted.

Examine your motives today. If there were persecution in your country would you still serve God?

Where Is Your Focus?

Think about the things of heaven, not the things of earth.
(Colossians 3:2NLT)

We sometimes become too focused on things that we should be trusting God to provide for us. He promises that just like he cares for the lilies of the field and the birds of the air he will provide got us in Matthew 6:25-30. If only we could fix our thoughts on applying the word of God to our lives and maturing as Christians. If only we could focus on developing fruit of the Spirit such as love, joy, peace and long suffering in our lives. If only we could love God with all our hearts and love our neighbors as ourselves. When we successfully achieve this aim we won't be attacked as much with stress related diseases. Stressors in your life can exacerbate all high blood pressure, diabetes, depression, headaches, asthma, and skin conditions. Philippians 4:8 NLT states "And now, dear brothers and sisters, one final thing. Fix your thoughts on what is true and honorable, and right, and pure, and lovely, and admirable. Think about things that are excellent and worthy of praise.

What have you been focused on lately, God's will or your own troubles?

Start Your Day With Prayer

My voice You shall hear in the morning, O Lord; In the morning I will direct it to You, And I will look up. (Ps. 5:3 NKJV)

Start your day with prayer. In the morning spend a little time with your heavenly Father. Set your alarm ten minutes early to thank God. Go to bed ten minutes earlier so you can wake up and cover your family with the blood of Jesus. If you don't get this done in the morning, Satan will for sure fill up your day so you'll have no time to pray later on. At night those of us with the best intentions usually fall asleep. Thank God for your health and strength and all He has given you, including your job, family, friends, shelter, and food. Ask for direction today and for the future. Ask Him to give you the opportunity to be a blessing. Ask Him to help you to understand His word. Let Him *hear* your voice in the morning.

What can you do to adjust your schedule so that you can spend time with God in the morning?

Cry Out to God

I cried to the Lord with my voice, And He heard me from His holy hill. (Ps. 3:4 NKJV)

We should cry out to God with our voices. If this idea embarrasses you, don't even think about it—instead just say it! God spoke creation into existence. He *said*, "Let there be light," and there was light. When tempted by the Devil, He *said,* "Man does not live by bread alone." When you're fighting depression, *say*, "The joy of the Lord is my strength." When you're fighting sickness, *say*, "By His stripes I was healed." When you're fighting financial problems, *say*, "My God will supply my every need according to His riches in glory." Use your voice—call to Him—and He will hear and act on your behalf every time!

When is the last time you spoke aloud to God? Jesus spoke to the devil when the devil tempted him, and he spoke when He prayed. Begin to speak God's powerful word aloud today and everyday.

Use Your Sword

But You, O Lord, are a shield for me, My glory, and the One who lifts up my head. (Ps. 3:3 NKJV)

Sometimes life is like a war that we feel we're losing. Don't just stand there and get beaten up! God is your shield. Stand knowing that He is there, in you. You don't have to worry about your defense—just your offense in this battle. Pull out your sword and fight. Your sword is the word of God. You won't be able to fight effectively, however, until you learn the word of God. Learn how to use your concordance for the verses you need to stand on. Memorize the Scriptures you need until they're not just in your head but also in your heart. Whatever battle you're facing, the good news is that you'll win. We shouldn't be negative or have defeatist attitudes. God lifts our heads because we have the victory!

What are some other weapons you can use in your spiritual battles?

Honesty

An honest answer is like a kiss of friendship. (Proverbs 24:26 NLT)

Honesty is a requirement for Christians. Our God does not lie and we are His children. We need to follow our father's footsteps. Usually we are tempted to lie because of our pride. We're concerned that the truth might not put us in the best light. Luke 6:45 NLT says "A good person produces good things from the treasury of a good heart, and an evil person produces evil things from the treasury of an evil heart". What you say flows from what is in your heart. What comes out of your mouth is what's in your heart, or what you actually believe. Integrity is essential. We should be people of our word. If we say we are going to do something, others should be able to count on us. Employers should feel that Christians are the best workers. Relationships are built on trust and honesty. We need to build relationships to show the love of God to a lost and dying world. Let's strive to represent our heavenly Father well. As pleasant as a friend's kiss is someone who is honest. Be known as a person of integrity, honesty and dependability, avoiding the temptation to lie at all costs.

How many people in your circle of friends would you say are people that demonstrate integrity? What would they say about you?

Don't Be A Fool

The way of a fool is right in his own eyes, but he who heeds counsel is wise. (Prov. 12:15 NKJV)

Sometimes we make serious decisions but don't ask God or anyone else if we're doing the right thing. We may erroneously think we've heard from God because the decision is what we want. The Bible calls a person who doesn't get godly counsel a fool. Getting counsel doesn't mean spreading your business around or asking unsaved family members or friends for advice. It means sharing your heart with someone who will pray to God and hear from Him on your behalf. Your desire already is confirmed in your heart, and now you're getting confirmation that it is *His* will for you. The way of a fool seems right in his or her own eyes.

Who do you go to for godly counsel?

Get Wisdom

Get wisdom! Get understanding! Do not forget, nor turn away from the words of my mouth. (Prov. 4:5 NKJV)

We can't let life deprive us of all God has for us. We won't know what's ours unless we read the word, study the word, and ask God to use the word to speak to us. Put God's word in your mind and your mouth, and above all, your heart. Does it take all that? Yes! The enemy is out to kill you, steal from you, and destroy you. Get the word of God, and start today.

When can you carve time out of your busy day to read the word of God?

_____

_____

_____

_____

_____

_____

_____

_____

_____

_____

_____

_____

Undeserved Blessings

So David said to him, "Do not fear, for I will surely show you kindness for Jonathan your father's sake, and will restore to you all the land of Saul your grandfather; and you shall eat bread at my table continually." (2 Sam 9:7 NKJV)

David wanted to bless Jonathan's son Mephibosheth because of David's love for Jonathan. Mephibosheth was crippled and had no one to work the land or care for him, but David said Mephibosheth would eat with him and be prosperous from that day forward. Because of our heavenly Father, we also receive blessings that we don't deserve. God's love of Jesus enables us to receive blessings all the days of our lives, just like Mephibosheth. It's not how hard you work or how much money you make but whom you serve that matters. God gives us the power to obtain both spiritual and financial wealth. Your relationship with Him blesses you and your children. Concentrate on developing your relationship with Jesus more than worrying about things you can't control.

What steps can you take today to develop your relationship with Jesus more?

Kill Your Giants

Your servant has killed both lion and bear; and this uncircumcised Philistine will be like one of them, seeing he has defied the armies of the living God. (1 Sam. 17:36 NKJV)

Trials arise to make you strong and prepare you for battles to come, and so that you may give God the glory. Remind yourself, as David did, of your previous victories. Has God helped you kill the lion and the bear in the past? Has He helped you overcome fears? Get a job? Get healed? Get out of debt? Heal your marriage? Pass a test? These obstacles were your lion and bear. Because of your past victories, you now are prepared to kill the giants you face, just like David did. This is why we can count trials as joys, because without them we wouldn't be victorious over the giants in our lives. Never forget what God has given you, because it strengthens your faith so that you can win the battles ahead.

What things in your past that Satan intended to harm you, have actually helped strengthen you to be the person you are today?

_____

_____

_____

_____

_____

_____

Make a Difference

But Ruth said: "Entreat me not to leave you, or to turn back from following after you; for wherever you go, I will go; and wherever you lodge, I will lodge; Your people shall be my people, and your God, my God." (Ruth 1:16 NKJV)

After Ruth's husband died, she could have gone back home to her people and their gods, but instead she chose to serve the God of her mother-in-law Naomi and stay with her. Naomi must have let her light shine with her daughters-in-law, loving them despite their backgrounds and customs. Let Naomi be our example today in a lost, dark world where so many people don't know Jesus. Love people so much that they become so close to Christ that they never want to serve the Devil again. Make a difference in someone's life, and God will bless you as He blessed Ruth. Because Ruth chose the God of Israel, she was blessed with a rich husband and a child who was in the family line of our Savior, Jesus Christ.

Are you letting your light shine?

Stop Doing Your Own Thing

Therefore take careful heed to yourselves, that you love the Lord your God. (Josh. 23:11 NKJV)

Joshua was an old man here, reminding the children of Israel of all the battles God had helped them win and of how faithful God had been to them. Let us remind ourselves every day of all God has done, giving us victory after victory, never leaving us alone. It's so easy to forget how God has blessed us when we have new mountains to climb, but God has gotten you this far. Love Him by obeying Him, learning His word, and listening to His still, small voice instead of doing your own thing. Never forget what He has done in your life!

What new mountains are you facing today? What old mountains has God moved for you?

You Can't Hide Anything from God

Get up, sanctify the people, and say, "Sanctify yourselves for tomorrow," because thus says the Lord God of Israel: "There is an accursed thing in your midst, O Israel; you cannot stand before your enemies until you take away the accursed thing from among you." (Josh. 7:13 NKJV)

Joshua was told to destroy the city of Ai and to bring the sacred gold and silver to the house of the Lord. Achan kept the gold and silver and hid them in his tent for himself. He was disobedient and kept what God told him to destroy. He was destined to face defeat with his enemies until he got rid of it. What are you holding on to that you know God has told you to give up? Do you socialize with the wrong people, drink alcohol, curse, read the wrong books or magazines, watch the wrong movies, or spend time in the wrong places? Sanctify yourself and give up these things so that you may be blessed in the midst of your enemies. We must care more about what God thinks than we care about what our friends and family think.

Are there things that you are hiding in your tent in disobedience to God?

Your Promised Land

For the Lord your God dried up the waters of the Jordan before you until you had crossed over, as the Lord your God did to the Red Sea, which He dried up before us until we had crossed over. (Josh. 4:23 NKJV)

God dried the Jordan River and parted the Red sea. Is there anything too big for God to accomplish? In the twenty-first century, He's still the miracle-working God from the Old Testament. Is a river, sea, or mountain blocking you from walking where God has put in your heart to go? Talk to God about it! He'll dry up the river, part the sea, and move the mountain when you ask and believe. Stop trying to make your own path when God wants to do it for you. Cross over into your personal promised land today!

What mountains are blocking your path to victory? List the obstacles in your way and pray about each and every one.

_____

_____

_____

_____

_____

_____

_____

_____

_____

He is God in Heaven and on Earth

And as soon as we heard these things, our hearts melted; neither did there remain any more courage in anyone because of you, for the Lord your God, He is God in heaven above and on earth beneath. (Josh. 2:11 NKJV)

This is Rahab the prostitute speaking. She had no one to preach the word to her. She had no Bible, but she heard about all the miracles that God had done for the Israelites and said that God is Lord in heaven and on earth. Because of her faith, she risked her life protecting the men of God. How much greater should our faith be when God has performed miracles in our own lives? We have the word; we go to church; and the Holy Spirit dwells in our hearts. Have the faith of Rahab. Never doubt the God we serve. He is still able, no matter what you're going through.

What areas of your life do you need to work on to strengthen your faith?

Temptation

For in that He Himself has suffered, being tempted, He is able to aid those who are tempted. (Heb. 2:18 NKJV)

Jesus walked on this earth as a man and was tempted by Satan, as we all are. Even so, He was able to live a sinless life, despite temptation. Now He is able to help us with temptation because He experienced it. He left heaven to become a man—yet still God—for us. That's how much He loves you and me. When sin knocks on your door and you're tempted, ask Jesus for help. He gives you the strength you need to live a life that pleases Him. Stop before you curse at someone, get angry, overeat, fornicate, become jealous or envious, or gossip. The list goes on and on, but with Christ you can do all things!

What has been your biggest temptation? What practical things can you do the next time you're tempted in order to remain strong?

Fight To Win

Fight the good fight of the faith. Take hold of the eternal life to which you were called and about which you made the good confession in the presence of many witnesses. (1 Tim. 6:12 ESV)

Yᵒᵘ may not have realized you're in a fight, a battle, but you are. If there's a good way to fight it, there's also a bad way or wrong way. We want eternal life, and the enemy wants us to go to hell. Wrong-way thinking means having a pity party when life strikes, not praying, getting ungodly advice, not going to church, and trying to do everything on your own. The good fight of faith means getting up every day expecting God to bless you. Having a positive attitude with your mind on the things of God—the word of God—is the good fight. Pray without ceasing, get godly counsel, and don't avoid going to church. Fight to win!

List a few things that you're willing to fight for today, which you'd previously given up on.

Conclusion

I hope that this book has been a blessing to you. Perhaps, you have not considered becoming a Christian before but are ready to make that decision now. My Pastor, Jim Cobrae, has a very aggressive altar call, which thousands of people have responded to because it's anointed by God. I would like to conclude with this invitation for you to accept Jesus as Lord and Savior of your life.

Many Americans think they're OK with God. They've been told that God loves them and cares for them, which is true, but they have not gone through the necessary steps for salvation. You can't get to heaven because you're friends with the Pastor. You can't get to heaven because your mom brought you to church and told you that you were saved.

If you were to get up right now and your heart stopped and you died, would you go to heaven or would you go to hell? Let's examine your answer.

Let's talk about those who answered that you think you would go to heaven..."I think I'd make it". Let me tell you what the bible says. Nowhere in the bible does it say, you can think your way into heaven. It doesn't say positive thinking will get you to heaven. I love you enough to tell you, you're not going to make it by thinking it. I respect you enough and honor you enough to stop playing religious games with you and tell you you're not going to make it, because somebody needs to tell you the truth.

Maybe some of you answered, "Well, I hope I'm going to make it" Nowhere in the bible does it say if you say, "I hope, I hope, I hope..." that you're going to make it to heaven. This is unlikely as, sitting in the garage and hoping you are a car, will make you a car. You're not going to make it by hoping.

Maybe you feel that because you love God, you're going to make it to heaven. Nowhere in the Bible does it say that you get to go to heaven and have eternal life if you love God. The guys that crashed into the World Trade Center, said that they loved God too. Wrong God, and the wrong kind of love caused them to go to hell. By simply saying that you love God doesn't make you a Christian and get you to heaven.

Maybe some of you are saying to yourself, "Well, I'm a pretty good person". Most Americans say they're going to heaven because they're pretty good and nice, and give their money to charity. Nowhere in the Bible does it say that being a good person gets you to heaven. We believe that being nice will get us to heaven, because perhaps we've seen it written in some movie script in Hollywood. However, by merely being a good person, you don't get to go to heaven. If you're going to get to heaven you must get to heaven God's way. Jesus said, "I am the way, the truth, and the life. No one comes to the Father except through me". *(John 14:6 NKJV)* so we'd better do it His way.

Maybe some of you answered the question; "My mom and dad told me I was a Christian when I was a kid. They said I wasn't a Buddhist, Muslin, Hindu and that I was born in America. America is a Christian country and that makes me a Christian. I was even christened or baptized as a baby. They put a cross or Saint Christopher around my neck and took me to catechism, Sabbath school or Sunday school classes to learn the word" Can you show me in the Bible where it says that that is how we get to go to heaven ...because your mom and dad told you that you were a Christian? It's not there. Can you show me in the Bible where wearing a cross or religious jewelry, or going to classes to learn the Bible, will get you to heaven and give you eternal life? It's not there. You're hoping to get there because your wonderful parents tried to teach you about God, but that isn't the way to get there. Somebody needs to love you enough to tell you the truth; you're not going to make it to heaven.

Maybe you answered, "Someone told me that if I believe that Jesus Christ is the Son of God then that makes me a Christian. I truly believe that Jesus is the Son of God so I am a Christian. The Bible says that demons believe that Jesus is the Son of God, but they're not Christians and they're not going to heaven. "You believe that there is one God. You do well. Even the demons believe—and tremble! *(Jas. 2:19)*. The fact that you have head knowledge of who Jesus is, or mental acknowledgement does not get you to heaven. Most Americans know who Jesus is but that doesn't make them Christians. We know of the baby born in a manger and have sung songs about him at Christmas, and then heard the stories at Easter, but that is only head knowledge. We've seen Charlton Heston in the Ten Commandments movie and know the story. We know who Jesus is, but it's not about what you have in your head, mental acknowledgement, it's about what you've done with your heart.

If we're going to get to heaven we have to do it God's way. In the third chapter of the book of John, Jesus comes to a man named Nicodemus. "What do you mean?" exclaimed Nicodemus. "How can an old man go back into his mother's womb and be born again?" Jesus replied, "I assure you, no one can enter the Kingdom of God without being born of water and the Spirit. *(John 3:4, 5 NKJV)* Nicodemus was probably better than all of us. Nicodemus was a keeper of the law, memorized the scripture, sang, quoted and debated the scripture. He fed the poor in his community, wore ecclesiastical robes and was a leader in his synagogue. Wouldn't you think that Jesus would say you're such a good man that you get to go to heaven? Jesus doesn't do that, but instead, comes to Nicodemus and tells him that he must be born again. Most people that attend American churches simply don't understand what "born again" means.

Born again means, from the beginning of the bible, to the end of the bible, God is after all of your heart and all of your life. You must give God all of your heart and all of your life. It's an all or nothing relationship. In the book of Revelation *(Rev 3:16)* Jesus says I'm coming back and when I come back, I'd better find you either hot or cold. If I find you lukewarm I will vomit you from my mouth. This is a warning to lukewarm people. He's saying that people who call themselves Christians, that are lukewarm, are not real Christians and are not going to make it to heaven. What's a lukewarm person? A lukewarm person is someone who's a little in, a little out, a little up, a little down, occasional prayers, not against God but never giving God all of their heart or all of their life. Even though you prayed those prayers as a child and are a pretty good person, you have to give God all of your heart and all of your life. He's not a thief to rob you, a conniver or a trespasser to take from you what is yours; because it's your heart and your life, you must give it to him. It's your call and your choice. Will you give him all your heart and all your life? Jesus says if you confess me before men, I'll confess you before my father, if you deny me I'll deny you. He's not a man that he can lie. You don't want Jesus in your head only, like most Americans, but you want to give him all of your heart and all of your life. If you've been running *from* God instead of *to* God, I'm speaking to you. If you've never given God all of your heart and all of your life, I'm speaking to you. Maybe you repeated a prayer by a television evangelist, which is wonderful, but God checks your heart with your words to see if what you prayed was sincere. There are no magic abracadabra words for salvation, but God sees if your life matches your words.

Are you ready? Will you choose today to give God all of your heart and all of your life?

Wherever you are, repeat this prayer, not just with your mouth, but also with your heart.

Sinner's Prayer

Father, I confess that I'm a sinner, please forgive me. I believe that Jesus is your son and that he died on the cross for my sins. I believe that He rose from the dead and lives today, seated at the right hand of God. I believe that I must be born again by giving you all of my heart and all of my life. I choose this day, to confess with my mouth and to believe in my heart that you are God. I believe Jesus was crucified for all of my sins, in order for me to have the opportunity for eternal life. I ask you right now to come into my life and be my Lord and Savior. I trust in you alone Lord, as my Lord and my God from this day forward. Thank you Lord for forgiving me and saving me. Thank you that my name is now written in the Book of Life and that I am born again. Thank you that I am now a Christian!

Congratulations, on making the biggest commitment of your life! Now, find a local church to begin learning the word, and fellowshipping with those of like faith.

The following scriptures support your salvation today:

That if you confess with your heart the Lord Jesus and believe in your heart that God raised him from the dead, you will be saved (Rom. 10:9 NKJV)

For all have sinned and fall short of the glory of God (Rom. 3:23 NKJV)

For God so loved the world that He gave His only begotten Son, that whoever believes in Him should not perish but have everlasting life (John 3:16 NKJV)

For by grace you have been saved through faith, and that not of yourselves; it is the gift of God (Eph. 2:8 NKJV)

Made in the USA
San Bernardino, CA
26 November 2014